KNOW YOUR FINANCE

KNOW YOUR FINANCE

ATUL DESHPANDE

™

Bigfoot Publications

Because, there's a writer in everyone.

Know Your Finance
Author : Atul Deshpande

First Published by
Bigfoot06 Publications (OPC) Pvt. Ltd.
B-10,12 Shree Shyam Palace,
Sector 4,5 Chowk, Old Railway Road,
Gurugram, Haryana (122001)
Website: www.bigfootpublications.in
Email: info@bigfootpublications.in

First Edition: July, 2023

ISBN Print Book **-978-81-19201-91-4**

Printed in India

TABLE OF CONTENTS

INTRODUCTION

While working in one of India's major banks, I had the opportunity to meet a diverse range of people. During my service, I was posted at various places, including rural, urban, and metro cities. This allowed me to interact with various individuals who held different views about money One striking observation I made was that many people earned a good amount of money but still struggled financially.When I thought about this problem, I realized that it's not entirely their fault. The main problem lies in the fact that we are never taught how to handle money. Our schools do not offer any courses on personal finance. We study subjects such as Science, Mathematics or Languages which prepare us for employment. However, once we start earning, many of us are clueless on how to handle our money and tend to make mistakes.

Money plays an important role throughout our lives, which is why financial education is important. But to my surprise, I did not find any book containing all the concepts of personal finance. This realization prompted me to write this book. My intention is to introduce readers to the practical aspects of financial world that we encounter in our day-to-day lives. As a banker, I have taken into account the relevant problems faced by the general public while writing this book. It is my sincere hope that, readers will find the information in this book to be both relatable and applicable to their own financial situations. I hope this book will serve as a guide to navigating the financial world, and help you achieve the goal of being FINANCIALLY INDEPENDENT.

Let's start the journey!

CHAPTER 1
COMPOUNDING

Sumit and Kishor are government employees working in the same office. They have salary accounts in a nationalized bank. Both of them needed a personal loan of Rs. 5,00,000 for some household work, so they visited the bank to enquire about the loan. Their bank was offering personal loan at an interest rate of 12% per annum. After enquiring about the formalities, they went back to the office. In the office, one of their colleagues informed them that a nearby finance company is offering personal loans with simple interest rate of 10% p.a. Upon hearing this, Kishor got excited and immediately rushed to the finance company's office. He availed the loan thinking that he has got a great deal. Sumit was not so sure about the finance company, so he applied for the loan at his bank with a 12% interest rate. Both had availed the loan for a period of 5 years.

After a few months, Kishor noticed that he was paying an EMI of Rs. 12500, whereas Sumit was paying an EMI of Rs. 11200. Kishor felt cheated and went to the finance company's office to enquire about it. The branch manager showed him the EMI calculations, which were correct. Kishor was puzzled as to how it happened that the simple interest EMI was greater than compound interest EMI.

You may be curious about how this happened, as we all have learned the same things in school, just like Kishor. Well, that is how people sometimes get deceived if they do not know the intricacies of the financial world. This book is attributed to make you aware of such intricacies so that your financial decisions should not go wrong. As far as the example is concerned, we will understand it in later chapters of the book.

I decided to take the first chapter on Compounding, as it is an integral part of every banking transaction, be it a loan or an investment. In compounding, the principal amount earns the interest, and that interest is reinvested to earn more interest. In investments, it works as a magic, and those who understand the power of compounding, can do wonders in their financial growth. How it happens, let's find out in detail.

We all have learned the formulas to calculate simple interest and compound interest. The formulas are as follows

For Simple Interest

$$S.I. = \frac{P*r*t}{100}$$

For Compound Interest

$$A = P\left(1+\frac{r}{100}\right)^t$$

Here the values are

P= Principal Amount (amount of investment)

r = rate of interest at which the investment grows

t = total time period or number of years

Assuming that we deposit some money each month in an investment product, let's see how these variables (P, r and t) affect the interest we receive upon maturity. For that purpose, I kindly request you to download any financial calculator on your phone, so that you can also compare the results.

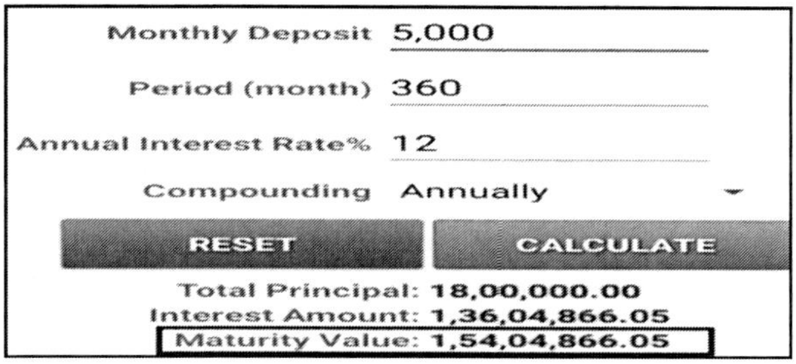

Image 1

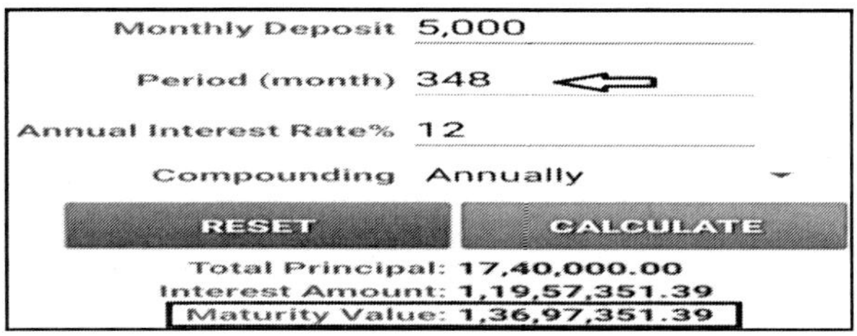

Image 2

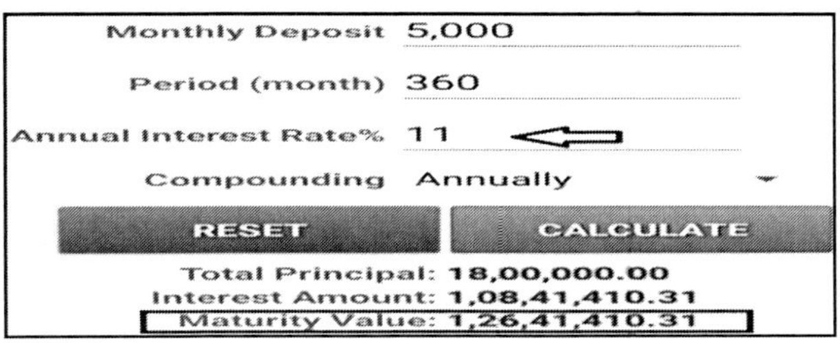

Image 3

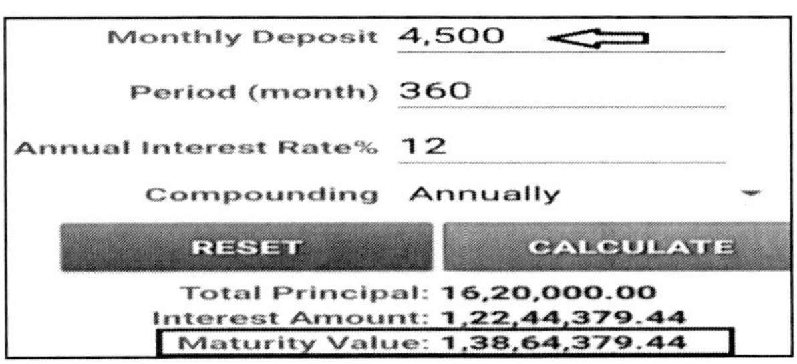

Image 4

As you can see in image 1, we have invested Rs. 5000 per month for 30 years fetching a rate of interest at 12% and our maturity amount is 1.54 crores at the end of 30 years.

Now as per our Compounding formula, if we change any variable the results would be different. As you can see in Image 2, we reduced the time period (t) of our investment by just one year, and our maturity amount drops to Rs. 1.37 crores. So we suffered a difference of Rs. 17 lakhs just in 1 year. If you look closely, you will notice that the total investment for 29 years is Rs. 17.40 lakhs, which means the total investment amount, would have been doubled in the last year.

In image 3, we invested the same amount (Rs. 5000) for the same period (30 years), but reduced the rate of interest (r) by just 1%. This resulted in reducing the maturity value to 1.26 crores, which is 28 lakhs lower than our original value.

And in image 4, we reduced our principal amount (P) by just Rs. 500 per month. Keeping it invested for 30 years at 12%, the maturity value decreased by 16 lakhs to 1.38 crores.

Now you must have understood that how each parameter plays an important role in compounding, Therefore, it is important to invest a sufficient amount every month (P) giving it proper time (t) to grow in products that offers good returns(r) on your investment. In the next chapter, we will explore different types of investment products along with the returns associates with it, so that you can plan your investments accordingly.

And if you check properly in every image, you will see that the original value of investment has grown nearly 8 times at maturity.

THAT'S THE MAGIC OF COMPOUNDING!!!

CHAPTER 2
INVESTMENTS

Ashwin is a software engineer working in Delhi. His father recently sold their ancestral agricultural land, and Ashwin received Rs. 20 lakhs as his share. Unsure of what to do with the money, he visited his bank and met Branch Manager Mr. Sachin, to seek investment advice. However, on the same morning, Sachin received a call from his boss, instructing him to sell insurance policies to achieve his monthly target. Seeing an opportunity, Sachin told Ashwin to invest the money in an insurance policy, which will fetch him the interest at the rate of 7 %, better than Fixed Deposits. Ashwin agreed, as he was unaware of any other investment options. He signed the papers, and the policy was issued to him a few days later.

This has become a common scenario in many bank branches as the customers are often clueless about the investment options. As a result, employees may try to push products based on their targets. Therefore, it is important for you to have a good understanding of investment products, enabling you to invest according to your needs. We will now explore the products which are available in Indian markets and try to understand the risk-reward ratio associated with each of them.

1 – **Fixed Deposit (FD)** –Popular among many people traditionally, it is one of the lowest risk products offering returns in the range of 3% to 7%. There are two types of FDs: one where you can receive monthly /quarterly interest and in the other type, you receive total interest at maturity.

2 – **Multi Option Deposit (MOD)** - Multi Option Deposit Scheme are term deposits linked to the savings account. It is basically a combination of a savings account and a fixed deposit where you can avail benefits of both. Usually, the interest rate of saving account is around 3% whereas fixed deposit rates are higher. However, you cannot withdraw money anytime from the fixed deposit. To avoid such inconvenience, this product is designed in such a way that you can receive higher interest rates and you are also able to withdraw your money anytime.

To understand how it works, let's consider you have a balance of Rs. 1,00,000 in your savings account. The bank will keep a threshold balance+ of Rs. 10,000 in your savings account and the remaining Rs.90,000 will be automatically converted into a fixed deposit (MOD) . If you do not withdraw that money for, let's say, 2 months, then you will earn the fixed deposit interest rate on that Rs.90,000. After two months if you withdraw Rs. 30,000, then the withdrawal will first be made from your savings account which has Rs. 10000, and then the remaining Rs. 20,000# will be withdrawn from your MOD account. As a result, your MOD balance will now be Rs.70,000. You will continue to earn higher interest on your MOD balance of Rs.70,000 till you withdraw again.

+Threshold balance is the amount above which the remaining balance goes into MOD. Threshold balance criteria may vary from one bank to another.

Rs. 20000 will be withdrawn and interest earned for 2 months will be deposited in the saving account. Unlike FDs, here withdrawal or transfer can be done instantly via ATM, Chequebook, INB, UPI etc.

You can convert your normal saving account into a MOD account by submitting an application at your bank branch. This product may have different names depending on the bank, such as flexi deposit, savings plus, sweep, etc. You can enquire about this option at your bank branch.

Trick – To get maximum benefits, you can club a MOD account with a credit card. By using your credit card to pay monthly bills, grocery and other shopping expenses, your money will remain in the MOD account for a longer period, and then pay the credit card bill on time. This way you can earn higher interest without paying any extra charges.

Both of the products mentioned above are part of banking schemes. Similarly, the Government of India also introduces schemes to promote saving habits among the public. These schemes are known as **National Saving Scheme (NSS)**. These schemes are supported by our central government, and the interest rates for such schemes are determined by the government, which may change according to government policies. The rates of interest mentioned in the following products are the latest as of April-2023. However, it is advised to check the current rates online before making any investments. There are various schemes under NSS; the prominent ones are PPF, SSA, KVP and NSC. We will try to understand them one by one.

3 – **Public Provident Fund (PPF)** – One of the most prevalent government schemes, PPF currently offers an interest rate of 7.1%. The scheme has duration of 15 years after which you can choose to close the account and withdraw the entire amount or extend it for one or more blocks of 5 years. The minimum amount of investment in a year is Rs. 500, while the maximum amount is capped at Rs. 1,50,000.

A partial withdrawal facility is given after completing 6 years where you can withdraw 50% of the balance amount. In certain cases, the account can be closed after the completion of 5 years if there is a serious medical emergency of the account holder or dependent family members. The account can also be closed in case the account holder wishes to pursue higher education. An interest rate penalty of 1% will be levied during such closures hence you will receive interest at the rate of 6.1% if the account is closed before maturity. The account can be opened by any Indian citizen in their name and also for minors with a guardian. The facility to open a PPF account is available at banks and post offices across India.

4 - **Sukanya Samriddhi Account (SSA)** – Launched in 2015, this scheme is aimed at raising the fund for the future education of girl child. Parents or natural guardian of a girl child can opt for this scheme right from her birth till she reaches the age of 10. Only one account can be opened for each girl child, and a maximum of two accounts can be opened in a single family (with an exception allowed for twins and triplets). The account can be opened with a minimum amount of Rs. 250, and maximum of Rs. 1,50,000 can be deposited in a year. Currently the rate of interest on SSA is 8%. The maturity period for the scheme is 21 years from the date of opening the account, but deposits can be made only for the first 15 years. However, the account will keep earning interest until maturity. Partial withdrawal of 50% of the balance amount can be done for the purpose of higher education or marriage when the girl reaches the age of 18 years. Premature closure of the account is permitted in the case of a serious medical emergency or in the event of the death of either the account holder or guardian.

For both PPF and SSA, documentary proof regarding higher education (such as college admission letter or fee receipt) or in the case of a medical emergency (doctor's certificate and other medical documents) needs to be provided while making a withdrawal from the account. The facility to open an SSA account is provided by banks and post offices across India.

5- **Kisan Vikas Patra (KVP) –** The primary objective of this scheme is to double your investment amount. Therefore, the maturity period will be linked to the interest rate. Here you can use the **Rule of 72** to calculate the maturity period. The rule is used to calculate the approximate time period to double your investment. The formula for the rule of 72 is as follows

$$\frac{72}{Rate of interest on investment}$$

The current rate of interest for KVP is 7.50%. Hence applying the rule of 72, the maturity period will be

$\frac{72}{7.50}$ = 9.6 = Nine Years and Six months

Unlike PPF or SSA, the interest rate at which you have bought the KVP remains fixed throughout the tenure. The minimum amount of investment in KVP is Rs. 1000 and there is no upper limit on the investment. The certificates of KVP are available in the denominations of Rs. 1000, 5000, 10000 and 50000. Physical certificates will be issued for your invested amount. Premature closure of KVP can be done after the period of 30 months from the date of issue of a certificate. KVPs can be purchased from Post Office across India.

6- **National Saving Certificate (NSC) –** The fourth and final scheme among NSS schemes, National Saving Certificate currently offers an interest rate of 7.70%. The minimum investment amount in NSC is Rs. 1000 to open the account, and there is no upper limit on investment. The maturity period is of 5 years, and premature closure is not allowed except in the event of the death of the account holder. The investment in this scheme is available in Post Office across India.

These were the four prominent products under national saving schemes. Apart from these, the government offers other investment products as well. Let's take a look at some of them.

7 – **Government Bonds / Government Securities (G-Sec)** - When you need money for your expenses, you can go to a bank to avail a loan and pay interest on the loan. Similarly, when our government needs funds for infrastructure development, it takes loans from the public by issuing government bonds and pays interest on them. Since it is a loan hence these products (bonds) are called **Debt Funds**. The Reserve Bank of India (RBI) issues these bonds. These bonds typically have a longer maturity period of 5 years or more. The interest rate on bonds is known as the coupon rate. Bonds are named in the format like **"7.17% GS 2029"**,which means 7.17% interest rate (coupon rate) will be paid on Government Security (GS) and the maturity year is 2029. Interest on government bonds is paid every 6 months into the investor's account until maturity, and the invested amount is returned on maturity.

These bonds can be purchased directly from RBI. To invest in government bonds, you need to open a RBI Direct Gilt (RDG) account by logging into the RBI site at https://rbiretaildirect.org.in . The online account opening process is quick and simple, and no fee is charged for opening and maintaining the account.

8- **Sovereign Gold Bond (SGB)** – One of the popular types of investment in our country is to invest in gold. As we know, the price of gold increases over time, so we choose to invest in it. However, there are some challenges associated with physical gold. We have to pay making charges and GST for jewellery and it should be kept in bank lockers or personal safes to prevent theft. Additionally, when we try to sell the gold, we do not get back the making charges which we have paid.

To overcome these challenges, there is an alternative called Sovereign Gold Bond. It is a type of Government Bond where the investment is made in Gold. So instead of buying physical gold, you can purchase gold bond at the same rate, and the government also pays interest on them. The interest on SGB is fixed at 2.5%, and the maturity period is 8 years. Premature withdrawal is allowed after the fifth year. The interest on bond is received at half-yearly interval.

To understand it better, let me share my example. I purchased few grams of SGB in May-2018 at a price of Rs. 3114 per gram. As of February- 2023, the price of gold has increased to Rs. 5600 per gram, resulting in a 79% increase in the investment amount. Along with this, I am also receiving interest on my investment at 2.5% p.a. every 6 months.

All these features make gold bond an attractive investment option. SGB can be purchased from banks, post offices, demat accounts and also from RBI RDG account. A discount of Rs. 50 per gram is offered to investors who purchase the SGBs online. The minimum investment amount in SGB is 1 gram, whereas the maximum amount is capped at 4 kilograms per person per year. Investment in SGB can also be made on behalf of a minor by their guardian.

All the products we discussed so far are considered low-risk products since they are backed by the government. Now we will move towards medium-risk and high-risk products. Low-risk products usually have a low rate of returns and as the risk increases there is a significant change in the potential returns. An investor should always have some part of his investment in low-risk products, and some part in medium and high-risk products. The underlying principle is that, your overall investments should be able to outperform the inflation rate. The products we discussed earlier offer returns in the range of 6-8%, while the current inflation rate is around 7%. So the overall investments should generate returns well above the inflation rate. Plus all these products discussed earlier have a lock-in period of some years so you will not be able to withdraw the funds. That is why some of your investments should be in such products which you can withdraw quickly for any emergencies. This is called liquidity. Hence, an ideal investment is a mix of products having balanced risk along with long and short-duration terms.

The returns on investment in medium and high-risk products are not fixed and there is always a possibility of loss in these products. So an investor should always have an understanding of risk management and strategies for risk mitigation. We will try to understand these products along with the risk associated with it and the ways to manage that risk.

9-**Stock Market or Share Market –** You might have seen a TV show called Shark Tank. In that show, investors come together to provide financial support to businessmen and in exchange for that, they ask for equity i.e. some percentage of ownership in their company. So in simple terms, equity means ownership. As and when the profit increases, the investors get a share of that profit as per their equity in the company. Share market is also called equity market because when you buy shares of some company you become a part owner of that company.

How share market works? Let's see with an example.

Mr. Mangesh is a businessman who owns a pipe manufacturing business named VM Industries in Maharashtra. He is running the business since last 10 years, and making a good profit every year. Recently he started receiving orders from other states, for which he thought it would be beneficial if he starts manufacturing plants in those states. He needs funds in the tune of Rs. 5 crore for the expansion. So he decides to raise the funds from public by listing his company on share market.

He does all the necessary paperwork with the share market regulator SEBI (Securities and Exchange Board of India) and obtains approval for the listing of his company. He then advertises about the listing, so that investors can buy the shares of his company. He intends to sell 1 lakh shares each having the price of Rs. 500. The shares are offered to the public for the first time hence it is called ***Initial Public Offering or IPO*** *and since the shares are available for sell for the first time, hence IPO is also called as* ***Primary Market.***

Once the company is successfully listed on stock market, people acquire shares and become shareholders. In the next year, the profit of VM Industries increases due to its new manufacturing units. Consequently more people become interested in purchasing those shares, as they see company can be in a good position in future. Since the demand of VM Industries shares is increasing, the price of the share keeps increasing. People are willing to purchase shares at higher price. Some of the people, who acquired the shares during IPO, decide to sell their share at higher price of say Rs. 600 to earn profit. In share market, people buy and sell shares to one another, hence it is called ***Secondary Market.***

So share market is basically a secondary market because people buy and sell shares to each other (Exchange). Price of shares fluctuates based on the performance of the company and various other factors. The total number of shares of a company multiplied by the price of each share is called ***Market Capitalization (M-cap)*** *of the company. In the case of VM Industries, there are 1 lakh total shares available in market, and price of each share is now Rs. 600, hence the market capitalization of VM Industries is Rs. 6 crores. If the share price falls to Rs. 400 then the market capitalization would decrease to Rs. 4 crores.*

As the profit of VM Industries grows in subsequent years, Mr. Mangesh decides to share that profit among the investors. The company declares that each of the shareholders of VM Industries will receive Rs. 50 per share they are holding. Such Distribution of profit among shareholders is known as ***Dividend,*** *which can become additional source of income for the investors.*

Investment in share market can be broadly classified into two types: trading and investing. In trading, people buy shares and sell them in short duration like on the same day or within a month. In investing, people buy shares and hold them for a longer duration of more than a year or sometimes a decade. Due to the volatile nature of share market in short term, trading is considered high-risk as compared to investing. Though trading can generate higher returns than investing but to generate decent profit with less risk, investing is preferred. There are two main share market indexes namely

a -Sensex (Short name for Stock Exchange Sensitive Index) is an index of the top 30 well-established and actively traded companies of India as per market capitalization. Sensex is also known as Bombay Stock Exchange (BSE).

b -Nifty (Short name for National Stock Exchange 50) also known as Nifty-50 is an index of the top 50 well-established and actively traded companies of India as per market capitalization. Nifty is also known as National Stock Exchange (NSE).

Investors can invest in both Nifty and Sensex as per their choice. A demat account is required to buy and sell shares on stock market, which can be easily opened online. The companies in Nifty are divided into following 3 categories as per the market capitalization.

a – Large Cap – The top 100 companies of the country, based on market capitalization, are called large cap companies. The market cap of these companies is more than Rs. 20,000 crores. These companies have an excellent track record and are considered stable for investment in long term.

b – Mid Cap – The next 101st to 250th companies, after large cap are called mid cap companies. The market capitalization of these companies is between 5000 crores to 20000 crores. These companies are more volatile than large cap but have a higher potential to grow and that is why these companies can provide higher returns than large cap companies.

c – Small Cap – Companies that rank from 251st and onwards are called small cap companies, having m-cap of less than 5000 crores. Though small cap companies can generate higher returns but these companies are considered extremely volatile for investment. A thorough research and analysis is required to invest in such companies.

Analyzing the historical performance of a product is an essential step for investors to make an informed decision. Similarly in share market, the study of historical and current performance of a company should be carried out before investing. Let's take a look at the historical performance of Nifty index and stock prices of some of the top companies of Nifty in last 20 years.

YEAR	NIFTY INDEX VALUE
2002	1075.4
2007	4082.7
2012	5199.25
2017	8561.3
2022	17339.85

COMPANY NAME	**STOCK PRICE IN JANUARY 2002**	**STOCK PRICE IN JANUARY 2022**	**GROWTH %**
RELIANCE	46.43	2386.6	5040
TCS	37.07	3111.35	8293
HDFC BANK	22.47	1485.7	6512
INFOSYS	60.58	1736.2	2766
HUL	220.7	2274.3	930
ICICI BANK	25.56	788.8	2986
SBI	19.81	538.3	2617
BAJAJ FINANCE	4.21	7000.25	166177
BHARTI AIRTEL	14.39	729.3	4968
ITC	15.43	220	1326

As you can see in both the images, long term-investments in stock market can generate remarkable returns. This happens due to a simple reason. The economy of a nation tends to grow in long term and as the economy grows, the companies start making more profit which in turn makes the share market and share prices to grow. However, following precautions should be taken while dealing in stock market.

a - Educate Yourself – You should get proper training regarding the workings of market. Educate yourself with well-recognized trainers before investing. You should learn about the fundamental and technical analysis of stocks in which you want to invest. Without adequate knowledge, there is a higher risk of losing money. You should start with low capital and invest in asmall number of large cap stocks initially to understand the working of market. Once you get confident then you can diversify your portfolio as per your choice.

b – Patience – One of the most important factors regarding market is to have patience. Though market keeps rising in long term, there can be short-term fluctuations where the market and the value of your investments may temporarily decline. During such time, you should have belief in your research and should not panic while dealing with such short term losses.

c – Buy the dip – Many people make the mistake of buying stocks when the market is at a high point and when market goes down, people cannot deal with the losses and sell their stocks. You should not make that mistake. Always buy stocks when the market is down, so that you will get the stocks at a lower price and keep holding the stocks till market goes up to generate profit.

d – Stock Selection – The stock price of large and mid cap companies are generally higher so people prefer to invest in small cap companies. These stocks are highly risky in nature. A good investor should always have a diversified portfolio where the major portion of their investment is in large and mid cap companies. A good investor should be able to do stock selection on their own and never rely on tips and unverified news.

If you follow all the rules and be vigilant about your investments then stock market can generate impressive returns which can help you achieve your investment goals.

10 – **Corporate Bonds-** As we have seen with the government bonds, when the government require funds, they issue government bonds for the public to invest in it. Similarly, when a company needs funds, it issues corporate bonds. In our example of VM Industries, when Mr. Mangesh wanted to raise money for the company, he sold his shares to the public. This means, he is not the 100% owner of the company as some percentage of shares is with public. In some cases, companies do not want to sell their shares, so they take loans from the public and issue bonds for that purpose. Just like government bonds, here the maturity period and interest rate are fixed while issuing the bond. Company pays the interest half yearly or annually and the initial amount is repaid at the end of the maturity period. Generally, corporate bonds offer higher interest rates than government bonds. These bonds can be broadly categorized in two types.

a – Secured Bonds – These bonds are secured by way of collateral. For example, when people take home loans, the bank takes their home as collateral security. If the borrowers fail to repay the loan, the bank can sell their home to recover the loan amount. Similarly, if the company fails to pay its bondholders, then bondholders can sell the collateral and recover their invested amount.

b – Unsecured Bonds – These bonds are not secured by collateral. For example- when people take personal loans, the bank does not take any security. If the borrowers fail to repay the loan, the bank cannot sell any collateral to recover the loan. However, banks still offer personal loans to public by looking at their salary amount, credit history and other relevant factors. Similarly, people invest in unsecured bonds looking at the previous history and track record of the company. Just as personal loans have higher interest rate than home loans due to the risk involved, similarly, unsecured bonds pay higher interest than secured bonds.

Unsecured bonds can also be referred as **Debentures.** You can purchase bonds via demat accounts or from various websites available in the market that deals in bonds.

11- **Mutual Funds (MF) –** We have seen different ways of investment like debt funds (bonds) and equity funds (stock market). However, it is not possible for everyone to do extensive research regarding which stocks to buy and when to buy them to generate maximum profit. In such cases, you can take the help of highly skilled professionals who has great experience in the financial world. These professionals do investments on your behalf and share the profit with you. This type of investment is known as Mutual Fund and the professionals who manage the investments on your behalf are called Fund Managers. There are various firms who collect the money from clients and invest it to generate profit. Such companies are called **Asset Management Companies (AMC)**, and the total amount of money collected from investors is called **Asset under Management (AUM).**

To avail these benefits, an investor needs to pay a certain percentage of their investment amount as a fee to this company. This fee is known as **Expense Ratio** and it is usually in the range of 1-2% of your investment amount.

There are various types of mutual funds as below

a – Large Cap Mutual Funds – As the name suggests, these funds invest a significant portion of their assets in large cap companies. These funds are considered stable for investment with low risk and low returns.

b – Mid Cap Mutual Funds – The major portion of the assets is invested in mid cap companies. These are medium-risk funds with higher returns than large cap funds.

c – Small Cap Mutual Funds – Here the major portion is invested in small cap companies. These are high-risk high returns funds.

d – Multi Cap Mutual Funds – In this fund, 75% of the assets are invested in large, mid and small cap funds equally (25% each). This is a diversified fund having exposure of all. These funds can generate higher returns in long term.

e – Debt Mutual Funds- As the name suggests, the major portion of this fund is invested in securities like government and corporate bonds and other fixed income securities. These mutual funds are also known as bond funds or income funds. These funds are less risky than equity funds so the returns can be less than equity funds. These funds are ideal for people who are risk averse as these funds are less volatile.

f – Balanced Mutual Funds - Also known as Hybrid Fund, the assets in this fund are invested in both equity and debt funds. As the equity portion of the fund provides higher returns, the bond portion ensures the stability of the fund. Hence the risk is minimized along with good returns.

g – Sectoral Mutual Funds- These funds focus on investing in a specific sector of the economy. The sectors can be Banking & Finance sector, I.T. sector or Pharma & Healthcare sector. Since the investment is done in any one sector of the economy, hence these funds are considered riskier as it lacks diversification. But some sectors come in demand during some event. For example- Pharma and Healthcare sector performed better during Covid-19 outbreak or I.T. sector performed better in I.T. boom, hence the profit can be generated if the investments are timed properly.

h – Equity Linked Saving Scheme (ELSS) Fund – The major portion of the asset is invested in equity or equity-related instruments. They offer the advantage of tax savings as the invested amount is eligible for exemption under section 80C of the Income Tax Act (up to Rs. 1,50,000), hence it is also called Tax Saving Fund. However, you cannot withdraw the amount before 3 years as this fund comes with a lock-in period of minimum 3 years.

g – Liquid Funds – This fund is for the people who want to park their surplus money and earn higher interest compared to regular savings account. Investors can park money in this fund for minimum 1 day and maximum up to 3 months. This fund is specially designed to provide liquidity to investors.

Except for ELSS, all other mutual funds provide you the facility of premature withdrawal, and it typically takes 2-3 working days for them to transfer the amount to your bank account. However, some mutual funds charge **Exit Load** if the amount is withdrawn before a certain period. Suppose you have invested in a mutual fund for 5 years, and their period for exit load is 1 year, then you will have to pay the exit load if you withdraw your amount before 1 year from the date of investment. Exit load is generally around 1% of the amount you are withdrawing.

Investments in mutual funds can be done in two ways: lump-sum or monthly investments. In lump-sum method, you invest a specific amount of money at once for a specific period, similar to fixed deposit. On the other hand, in the monthly method which is known as **Systematic Investment Plan (SIP)**, you invest a certain amount of money on a monthly basis and depending upon the market conditions, you are allotted units of that mutual fund every month. So when the market is down, you receive more units as compared to months when market is up. This way your investment gets averaged, resulting into bringing good returns over time. You can invest in mutual funds through various channels such as banks, demat accounts, or mutual fund websites/apps.

Suppose you invest through a bank, then an employee there will guide you regarding the mutual fund schemes of that particular bank. You will choose the scheme as per your need and the employee would collect your KYC documents to create a folio number for your mutual fund. This method is known as **Regular** way of investing. However, if you have done your own research and selected the mutual fund scheme independently, you can do the KYC procedure at the official website of that fund and the folio number will be generated. This method is known as **Direct** way of investing. The key difference between the two methods lies in the expense ratio. In regular funds, the expense ratio is higher because the bank acts as an intermediary/agent for the mutual fund company. The mutual fund company pays a commission to the bank from your expense ratio. Hence regular funds has higher expense ratio than direct funds. The difference can be of 1% or more. As we have seen in chapter 1 on compounding, even a difference of 1% in your returns can significantly impact your final amount. You can save this cost by investing through the direct method. Following precautions should be taken while investing in mutual funds.

a – Decide the type of mutual fund based on your risk-taking ability. Equity schemes have high risk and high return whereas debt schemes have low risk and low return. You can make your portfolio balanced by allocating funds as per the risk of the scheme.

b – Always look for the historical returns of the scheme. You can check the scheme performance on internet of last 1 year, 5 years, 10 years and overall performance since the inception of the scheme.

c – Your investments should be aligned with your goals. Goals can be short-term such as purchasing a car, or long term, such as building a retirement fund. So your scheme performance and risk ratio should be in line with your goals. Utilize the power of compounding to maximize the returns.

d – Always check the details like expense ratio, exit load period, and any such other charges as well as the terms and conditions of the scheme.

By considering these precautions and conducting thorough research, you can make informed choices when investing in mutual funds, helping you to achieve your financial goals effectively.

12 – **Nifty BeES –** Short name for Nifty Benchmark Exchange traded Scheme, is an instrument that replicates the performance of Nifty-50 index. In mutual funds, AMCs collects money from investors and invest it in different stocks. Similarly, in nifty bees, funds are collected from investors but instead of investing in a few stocks, the funds are invested in all the 50 companies of Nifty-50. So in simple terms, you are buying all the stocks of nifty-50 at a very low price. The price of bees is roughly $1/100^{th}$ of the Nifty index value. So if Nifty is currently trading at 17,000, then price of Nifty bees will be around Rs. 170 for a single unit. The price will increase or decrease as per nifty performance. As we have seen in stock market, the value of the Nifty-50 in 2002 was at 1075, which increased to 17,339 by the year 2022, making a growth of 1500%. Hence, nifty bees can become stable investments for the long term generating good profits. It is exchanged like stocks on stock market, hence it is also known as **Exchange Traded Fund (ETF).**

13 – **Real Estate Investment Trust (REIT)** – A new concept for Indian markets, REIT works as mutual fund for real estate. Here the asset management companies are called trusts. These companies buy the income-generating properties (malls, warehouses, office spaces) from your money and give it on rent. The rent which they collect is then distributed among the investors. The shares of REITs are traded on the share market and you can do the investment from your demat account. Real estate is a costly investment but REIT offers diversification to your investment portfolio in real estate with low

capital and without the hassle of owning and managing the property. These investments are also known as **Alternative Investments.**

14- **National Pension System (NPS) –** It is a voluntary defined contribution pension system launched by the government of India. The scheme was launched initially for government employees but later it was opened for all. Anyone who falls under the age of 18-65 years can invest in the scheme. The scheme is divided into two parts: Tier 1 and Tier 2. First, we will understand how the scheme works for tier 1 account.

NPS, as the name suggests is made solely for the purpose of giving pension at the time of retirement or resignation. The minimum amount of investment in a year is Rs. 500 and there is no upper limit for investment. As there is a fund manager in a mutual fund, there is a pension fund manager (PFM) in NPS to invest your money. The money is invested in 4 asset classes which are as follows.

Asset class E - Equity and related instruments (stock market etc.)
Asset class C - Corporate Bonds and related instruments
Asset class G - Government Bonds and related instruments
Asset Class A - Alternative Investment Funds including instruments like REIT and others

You will be given two options for asset management namely: Active choice and Auto choice.

a – **Active Choice** – In this option, you can personally decide the allocation percentage of your funds in different asset classes. Active choice is suited for investors who want to have control over their investments hence they can set the asset allocation as per their choice and risk capacity. Investors who want higher returns with higher risk can allocate maximum fund to equity instruments (asset class E), whereas investors who wants moderate returns with less risk can allocate their fund in debt instruments (asset class C &G). Based on your allocation, the pension fund manager will handle the investments.

To ensure that NPS should not become a high-risk product, the government has laid down some rules which have to be followed while allocation of funds. These rules are as follows

i- Maximum Equity Allocation – Until you reach the age of 50, you can invest a maximum of 75% of your funds in equity instruments (asset class E). This means the remaining 25% of your funds must be allocated to other asset classes (asset classes C, G, and A).

ii- Decrease in Equity Allocation – after turning 50, the maximum allocation to equity will be decreased by 2.5% per year. For example, at the age of 51, the maximum equity allocation can be 72.5%, at 52 it will reduce to 70% and so on. This rule ensures that exposure to equity (risk) should be reduced as the investor is approaching retirement age.

iii- Maximum Allocation in AIF- The allocation in alternative investment funds (asset class A), cannot exceed 5% of your total investment at any given time.

b – **Auto Choice –** For those subscribers who do not want to manage their investment, NPS offers an easy option of auto choice. In this option, the investment decisions are automatically managed based on predefined patterns. These patterns are called Life Cycles. There are three lifecycles and they are named as per the nature of the investment pattern they follow:

i – Aggressive Life Cycle (LC 75) – In this lifecycle, the maximum equity investment will be 75% till 35 years of age and it will be reduced by 4% each year onwards. So maximum equity investment at age 36 will be 71% and will continue to decrease accordingly. The remaining fund will be invested in other asset classes (C, G & A).

ii – Moderate Life Cycle (LC 50) - In this lifecycle, maximum equity investment will be 50% till 35 years of age and it will be reduced by 2% each year onwards.

iii – Conservative Life Cycle (LC 25) - In this lifecycle, maximum equity investment will be 25% till 35 years of age and it will be reduced by 1% each year onwards.

Subscribers can choose any of the lifecycles as per their risk capacity. NPS also provides the option of changing your choice of investment. You can change from active choice to auto choice or vice versa. The changes can be made twice in one year. Subscribers also have the option of changing their fund manager which can be done once in a year. Many state government and central government employees are covered under this scheme in which their employers also make a contribution to this scheme. Corporate employees can also avail the scheme and their employers can do contributions to the scheme.

The maturity age of NPS 60 years. At maturity, you can withdraw maximum 60% of the total amount in lump sum. The remaining 40% will be given to you in the form of monthly pension (annuity). Partial withdrawal is permitted in the following cases

i) Critical illness, higher education, or marriage of children – The maximum amount of withdrawal will be limited to 25% of your own contribution. Such withdrawal can be done after completion of 3 years from the date of opening the account.

ii) Premature Exit – In case of resignation from company or any other such cases, maximum 20% of the corpus can be withdrawn and remaining 80% will be provided in the form of monthly pension. Such withdrawal can be done after completion of 5 years from the date of opening the account. If the total corpus is less than Rs. 2.5 lakhs, subscribers can also opt for 100% lump-sum withdrawal.

All the information we discussed till now is the part of tier-1 account. To provide more flexibility for investment, an add-on account facility is provided which is called tier-2 account. In tier-2 account, you can withdraw the amount at any time and there is no restriction on withdrawals. However, an active tier-1 account is required to open tier-2 account. NPS account can be opened in banks or through its authorized website https://npscra.nsdl.co.in

15 – **Crypto-currencies –** Introduced in 2009, crypto-currencies are digital or virtual money that can be exchanged on a computer network. They exist in the form of coins. There are various crypto-currencies or coins which are available for exchange. Since there is no central authority to control these coins, hence it is also called decentralized currency.

The first such digital currency launched was Bitcoin. The price of one bitcoin in 2009 was less than Rs. 100, whereas in 2021 the price soared to Rs. 51,00,000 per coin. No other investment has given such whopping returns in recent times. Since it's a new type of investment and the market is unsure about its future hence it is a very high- risk investment. Nevertheless, it should be explored as this is a new-age digital investment and it can give amazing results. So it is advised to invest a little capital in such instruments so that you do not miss out on returns.

You should also keep exploring other such new avenues as we never know which one could become the next bitcoin. Some such avenues are NFT (Non-Fungible Tokens) which deals in digital art and Decentraland (MANA) which deals in digital land. There are various apps available to invest in these products.

With this, we conclude the chapter on investments. I have tried to give a brief and basic idea about the various investment products available in the financial market. Readers are encouraged to do a detailed analysis of the products in which they want to invest. This way you can take better decisions regarding the investments and can have a smooth journey in the financial world.

CHAPTER 3
LOANS & ADVANCES

Vivek and Nilesh have retired from their respective jobs this month. They were childhood friends who lived in the same city. Both of them had taken home loans of Rs. 50 lakhs. Nilesh had taken the loan for 20 years, whereas Vivek had taken it for 30 years. Nilesh had opted for a shorter loan period to reduce the interest amount, while Vivek used a different trick to save on interest. When he shared the trick with Nilesh, Nilesh was truly impressed. So, what was the trick Vivek used? Let's find out in this chapter.

Before we move on, first we will take a look at some of the basic terminologies which will help us to understand the chapter.

i) Gross Monthly Income (GMI) – The total salary you earn before the deduction of taxes and other mandatory deductions.

ii) Net Monthly Income (NMI) – NMI is the salary which gets deposited in your account. It is also called take-home pay.

iii) Equated Monthly Instalment (EMI) – It is the payment amount on the loan made by the borrower to the bank each month on a set date. The EMI includes both principal and interest.

iv) Tenure – The period for which the loan is availed.

v) Salary Package Account – It is a special saving account offered to salaried customers which provides unique benefits and services. There are various types of salary packages such as Defence Salary Package (DSP), State or Central Government Salary Package (SGSP or CGSP) and Corporate Salary Package (CSP).

vi) Collateral Security – Whenever you avail a loan, banks ask for an asset as a security which they can sell in case you fail to repay the loan. Like in a car loan, your car is the collateral security.

vii) Margin – Whenever you take a loan to purchase something, the bank does not give 100% loan of the value of that asset. The remaining amount you pay as a down payment is called margin. For example- if you are buying a house worth Rs. 50 lakhs, then the bank will give you 80-90% of the loan and you have to pay the remaining margin for that loan.

viii) Electronic Clearing System (ECS) –It is an electronic mode of payment of the EMI. ECS helps you to automatically pay the EMI from your saving account to your loan account on the set date every month.

ix) Processing Fee –It is the fee you have to pay when you avail a loan. It is calculated on the loan amount which is usually 0.50% to 2% of loan amount.

x) Prepayment/Foreclosure charges – If you close/prepay the loan before the stipulated tenure then the bank may charge a certain fee as a penalty which is called foreclosure charges. These are usually in the range of 2-4% of loan amount or outstanding balance of loan amount.

xi) Fixed Rate – If the rate of interest on your loan is constant through the entire tenure, it is called fixed rate. For example, if you availed a loan at 7% for 5 years, then the rate will not change until the completion of 5 years.

xii) Floating Rate – If the rate of interest on your loan keeps changing during the loan tenure, it is called floating rate. For example, if you availed a loan at an initial interest rate of 7% for 5 years, then the rate may change (increase or decrease) as per bank's instructions during these 5 years.

xii) Flat Rate – In this method, the interest is calculated on the initial loan amount and it remains the same throughout the tenure of the loan.

xiv) Reducing Rate – In this method, the interest is calculated on current outstanding loan amount.

In chapter 1 on compounding, we have discussed the example of Sumit and Kishor. Let's revisit that example once again to understand it better. In that example, both of them availed the same amount of loan for the same tenure but Kishor was paying more EMI than Sumit. The reason is Kishor's loan was under flat rate method, whereas Sumit's loan was under reducing rate method. Let's see how that happens.

In flat rate, simple interest formula is used to calculate the EMI. So the total interest for Kishor on his 5 lakhs loan at 10% will be

$$\textbf{Interest} = \frac{500000*10*5}{100} = \textbf{2,50,000}$$

The total amount to be repaid by Kishor including principal and interest will be 750000. The amount will be equally divided into 60 instalments; therefore the EMI amount will be Rs. 12,500.

Sumit, on the other hand, has opted for a loan with a reducing rate method, where compounding interest will be applied. We can calculate his EMI using a financial calculator.

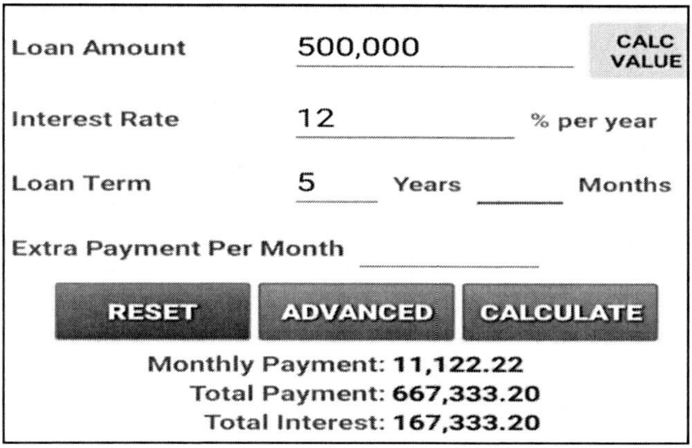

Image 1

As you can see the EMI amount is Rs. 11,122. The difference is due to the fact that in reducing method, the interest is calculated on the outstanding balance of the loan. For example, if you have taken a loan of Rs. 5 lakhs and you pay Rs. 1 lakh, then the interest will be applied only on the remaining Rs. 4 lakhs. So, when you pay EMI which consists of principal and interest, your outstanding balance keeps reducing each month and your interest amount also keeps reducing each month. However, in the flat rate method, even after paying Rs. 1 lakh, the interest will still be applied on Rs. 5 lakhs. This is why the flat rate of 10% is more than reducing rate of 12%. That is one of the benefits of compounding in a loan. Usually, government/ private banks use the reducing rate method, whereas some finance companies use the flat rate method while giving the loan. You should always check such details before availing the loan.

Now let's take a look at the different kinds of loans available in market.

1- **Loan against Deposit** – Suppose you have a fixed deposit of Rs. 10 lakhs in a bank having a 6% interest rate. For some short-term emergency, you need Rs. 1 lakhs. So, you have the option of closing the FD and withdrawing the funds. However, when you close the FD prematurely, there is an interest penalty of 0.5 – 1%. Instead of doing that, there is another option of taking loan on your FD. The rate of interest on the loan is usually 1% above the FD rate, which means if you are getting 6% interest on total FD amount of Rs. 10 lakhs then the rate of interest, will be 7% on your loan of Rs. 1 lakh. In this way, you don't have to close the FD and miss out on the interest. You can avail a loan of up to 85-90% of your FD amount and the tenure of the loan depends on the tenure of your FD.

The loan can be availed in the form of Overdraft (OD). Normally when you take a loan, banks disburse the total loan amount in your saving account, and you start paying EMI on it from the next month. This is called Term Loan (TL). However, with an overdraft, you can withdraw the loan amount in tranches, and you have to pay interest on the withdrawn amount only. For example, if you avail a loan of Rs. 1 lakh in the form of OD and withdraw Rs. 40,000, then you have to pay interest on that 40,000 only. As and when you withdraw more amounts, you will be charged interest according to that. Hence, OD works like a saving account where you can withdraw and deposit money as per your choice.

You can avail this loan on various deposits such as PPF and NSC, as discussed in chapter 2 under NSS schemes. However, there is no loan facility available against SSA and KVP.

2- **Personal Loan (PL) –** It is an unsecured loan that can be used for any personal purpose. Banks usually offer this loan to salaried employees or to the account holders who have good transaction history in the bank. The rate of interest on this loan can vary from 9% to 15% across different banks. Since banks do not ask for any collateral security which makes it an unsecured loan, hence the rate of interest is higher than other loans. The tenure for this loan is maximum of up to 6-7 years. Banks may charge prepayment/foreclosure charges of up to 2-4% if the loan is closed before specified tenure. Retired employees who receive pensions can also avail similar type of loan, which is known as a pension loan.

The amount of loan offered by the bank depends on your income. The eligibility for a loan is calculated by EMI/NMI ratio which is usually 50%. For example, if your monthly take-home salary (NMI) is Rs. 25000, the bank will give you the loan where your EMI should not exceed 50% of NMI i.e. Rs. 12500. The EMI here is a total of all the loans which you have availed and are currently running. So if you have already taken a loan where you are paying the EMI of say Rs. 5000, you are now eligible for the loan with an EMI up to Rs. 7500 (12500-5000). You can calculate your loan eligibility with the help of this ratio.

3- **Car Loan –** You can avail this loan to purchase a new car. Bank offers an 80-90% loan on the ex-showroom price of the car, as per your eligibility. The rate of interest varies between 8-11% and the tenure is usually up to 7 years. The loan can be availed by salaried individuals, businessmenen, self-employed individuals, and agriculturists as well. The loan can be taken in a single name or jointly with a family member. A joint borrower is called co-borrower, who can be added if the single borrower is not able to fulfil income criteria as per EMI/NMI ratio.

You can also avail a car loan to purchase a pre-owned (old) car. The interest rate for such loans is higher, ranging from 10-14%. A quality test is conducted to determine the residual life of the vehicle, and the tenure of the loan is decided based on that report.

Collateral security for this loan is your car, which will be used to secure the loan. This security is called hypothecation which will be recorded on your RC book and insurance papers. Once the loan is paid off, the bank issues a No-Dues certificate. This certificate is used to remove the hypothecation.

4- **Gold Loan-** This loan is offered against the gold ornaments as security. This security is called as pledge. The rate of interest on these loans is usually 7-9%, and tenure is usually up to 3 years. Banks have their appointed gold appraisers who check the quality and weight of the gold and determine the market value of gold. You can get a loan of 75-80% of that market value. This loan is favoured by many people for the following reasons:

i) Low interest rates.

ii) Easy loan process with less documentation.

iii) Convenient repayment schedule- You can pay this loan in EMIs or as a lump-sum at the end of the tenure.

iv) Safety of ornaments- When you avail the loan, the bank keeps your gold in their custody, providing a safer option for your ornaments until the loan is fully repaid.

v) No foreclosure charges – Usually, there are no foreclosure or prepayment charges on gold loans.

If you have agriculturalal land in your name, some banks offer agriculture gold loans where the interest rates are lower than normal gold loans. You can check with your bank for such schemes and compare the rates. When availing a gold loan, it is necessary to check the interest rates mentioned. Rates can be expressed as per annum (p.a.) or per month (p.m.). All the rates we discussed here are in p.a. If the rate is mentioned as p.m., you should multiply it by 12 to arrive at the p.a. rate. For example, a 0.75% p.m. rate is equivalent to 9% p.a. rate. This loan can also be availed against the Sovereign Gold Bond (SGB), which was discussed in chapter 2.

5- **Education Loan** - The loan is aimed at providing financial assistance to students for pursuing higher education in India and abroad. Any student who wishes to pursue higher education can avail this loan, subject to the terms and conditions of the scheme. Education loan can be categorized into two parts: unsecured and secured loans. Let's understand them one by one.

a- Unsecured Education Loan – Loan up to Rs. 7.50 lakhs is considered unsecured loan as there is no requirement to provide any collateral security. A course that leads to diploma or degree is covered under an education loan. Students can apply for the education loan, and the parent will act as the co-borrower for the loan. In cases where parents are not available, natural guardians /grandparents /siblings /relatives or any other third party can act as the co-borrower.

The interest rate for the loan is in the range of 8-11% and the tenure can be up to 15 years after the moratorium period. The moratorium period is a period during which the student is not required to pay EMI on the loan. However, the interest is charged by the bank during moratorium period. Since the student is not able to repay the loan during the course period and sometimes may require time to find a job, hence moratorium period is given as the course period plus one year. For example, if a student is pursuing 3-year course, then the total loan tenure can be calculated as: course period (3 years) + moratorium period (1 year) + repayment period (15 years) which equals to 19 years. The loan can be availed before the beginning of the course or during any year of the course to fund the remaining duration of the study. Here are the salient features of the education loan

i- The expenses covered under the education loan include tuition fees, hostel fees (lodging and boarding), uniform, equipment and a laptop/computer if required for the completion of the course. Other expenses such as exam fees, library fees, books and project work are also considered.

ii- If a college does not have a hostel facility and student has to find accommodation elsewhere, the cost of accommodation can also be covered under the loan. Such costs are determined based on the prevailing lodging and boarding (room and mess) rates in that area.

iii- If the distance between the college and the hostel is too far, the facility to purchase two-wheeler is also provided in the loan up to a certain amount.

iv- Student can change the course or college if they get a better opportunity. Bank should be informed regarding such change and necessary documents should be provided.

v- If, for any reason, a student has already paid the fees and did not avail the education loan, they can apply for loan later, and the fees already paid can be reimbursed to them. There is a specific time period for such reimbursements (usually around 6 months). The receipts of such expenditures need to be provided for reimbursement.

vi- The bank will verify the CIBIL report of the student as well as the co-borrower. If the co-borrower does not have required CIBIL score, it is possible to change the co-borrower for the loan to get sanctioned.

vii- If the student has completed their course and wants to pursue higher studies, the bank should be notified of this decision. The bank will extend the moratorium period of the loan by the new course period. Student can also apply for loan for these higher studies.

b- **Secured Loan-** Education loans above Rs. 7.50 lakhs are classified as secured loans, as you have to provide a collateral security while availing the loan. The security can be in the form of land, house, fixed deposit, government bond, insurance policy, etc. The loan amount is decided based on the value of the security provided. Apart from this requirement, all the other features remain the same as an unsecured education loan.

However, for some premier and reputed colleges in our country, there are some exceptions regarding collateral. Such loans are known as scholar/premier/special education loans. For these loans, the requirement of collateral security is waived till a certain limit depending on the college. For example, some banks offer up to Rs. 40 lakhs loan without collateral for certain colleges. These premier colleges include IITs, IIMs, NITs, XLRI, BITs, and others. The list of such colleges is furnished by banks on their website.

Banks also provide education loan for studying in foreign institutes. Such loans are known global/foreign education loans. Students can apply for such loan if they have been offered admission by foreign institutes. Students can add the travel expenses (flight tickets to foreign nation) in the loan amount. All the other formalities remain the same as normal education loan.

The Government of India has developed an online portal for the students seeking education loans. This portal is called Vidya Lakshmi Portal (VLP). Students can login in to the portal and submit an education loan form online. Students can apply to their preferred bank branch from this portal. The portal can be accessed from https://www.vidyalakshmi.co.in.

Along with this, the Government of India is running various subsidy schemes to assist students. Two prominent schemes are as follows

i- Central Sector Interest Subsidy (CSIS) – This scheme is applicable to students whose family income is up to Rs. 4.50 lakhs. Under this scheme, the interest on the education loan during moratorium period (course period plus 1 year) will be paid by the government. After the moratorium period is over, remaining loan amount need to be paid by the student. The scheme is now renamed as Pradhan Mantri Uchchatar Shiksha Protsahan (PM-USP). The details of the scheme can be found on the portal https://www.jansamarth.in .

ii- Dr. Ambedkar Central Scheme of Interest Subsidy – Students who belong to Other Backward Class (OBC) or Economically Backward Class (EBC) are eligible under this scheme. The annual income of the family should not exceed Rs. 8 lakhs. This subsidy is available for OBC and EBC students pursuing higher education (Masters Degree, M.Phil. or PhD) in *foreign universities* only. Here also, the interest charged during the moratorium period will be paid by the government. The details of the scheme can be found on the portal https://canarabankcsis.in/ACSIS .

In addition to these schemes, there are various other subsidies available for students. The details can be obtained from the government website https://www.education.gov.in . The features of education loan may vary from one bank to another. Students are advised to check the eligibility criteria from the bank's authorized website or by visiting the bank's branch before applying for the loan. With this, we will now move on to home loans.

6- **Home Loan –** It is everyone's dream to own a house, and usually, it happens just once in our lifetime. Therefore, it is essential to have a good understanding of home loans. Luckily I have spent a considerable amount of time in loan department and have sanctioned more than 2000 home loans, so we will discuss this topic in great detail. Home loans are usually provided for the following purposes:

i) **Plot plus Construction** – If you want to purchase a plot and subsequently construct the house on it, the bank will give a loan for both the purposes. There is a specified time period, usually 3-5 years, in which the construction of the house should be completed after purchasing the plot on loan. If you already have a plot and want to construct a house, bank financing is also available for the construction.

ii) **Purchase of house** – A home loan is available to purchase either an old or a new house or flat.

iii) **Repair or Renovation** – If you have an existing house/flat and want to repair or renovate it, the bank provides loan for such expenses. If you are purchasing an old house/flat, and that house/flat requires repairs/renovation, you can also include that cost of repairs and renovation to enhance the loan limit.

A home loan can be availed by salaried individuals, businessmen, agriculturists, self-employed individuals who have a steady source of income. Your house /flat /plot is kept as collateral security while taking the loan. This security is called mortgage of the property. The rate of interest on home loans ranges from 7-11 % and the maximum tenure can be up to 30 years.

The amount of the loan is determined by two factors: LTV ratio and EMI/NMI ratio. In LTV (Loan to Value) ratio, the loan amount is decided by the value of the property. Banks evaluate the current market value of the property through their panel engineers. As per the value, the LTV ratio is as follows

Loan amount	LTV ratio
Up to 30 lakhs	> 80 and ≤ 90 %
above 30 lakhs and 75 lakhs	≤ 80 %
above 75 lakhs	≤ 75 %

For example, if the value of the property is Rs. 60 lakhs, you can avail loan of up to 80%, which amounts to Rs. 48 lakhs. You have to pay remaining Rs. 12 lakhs as margin money.

The other factor that determines your eligibility is EMI/NMI ratio. Your net monthly income from all sources is considered to calculate the eligible loan amount. Banks usually offer 30 -70% of EMI based on your salary. Let's understand this with an example:

Assuming your monthly take-home pay (NMI) is Rs. 50,000 and the bank provides an EMI/NMI ratio of 60%. Considering the current interest rate of the home loan as 7.50%, and you are taking a loan for 30 years, the EMI for Rs. 1 lakh will be Rs. 700 (you can verify this using a financial calculator). Based on your salary, your eligible EMI will be 60% of Rs. 50000 which amounts to Rs. 30000. Dividing this by 700, your final eligibility will be Rs. 42.85 lakhs.

The loan eligibility can be increased by adding a co-borrower who is having a steady source of income (salaried / businessman etc). You can add 2-3 such co-borrowers from the family members such as spouse, sibling, parents and children. Other income such as house rent, agriculture income can also be added to increase your loan eligibility (proofs of such income need to be furnished while availing the loan).

There are various other types of home loans which are as follows:

a – **Top Up –** In case you already have a home loan and require additional funds for any personal reasons, you can apply for top-up loan on your existing home loan. The concept behind top-up loans is that, as the value of the property increases over time, while the outstanding home loan amount decreases, so banks can use the difference to give top-up loans. These loans are considered low-cost loans since the interest rate is usually 0.50% above the current home loan rates, which makes it suitable for fulfilling short-term financial needs of the borrower.

b – **Take Over or Transfer of loan –** You have the option to transfer your home loan from one bank to another. People usually choose to do this for the following reasons:

i) Higher Interest Rates: If your current bank is charging higher interest rates, you can transfer the loan to another bank that offers lower rates.

ii) Tenure Extension: If you have taken a loan with a short tenure and wish to increase the repayment period, you can transfer the loan to a bank that allows for a longer tenure.

For these and various other reasons, people opt to transfer their home loans to another bank. This transfer can be done after completing one year with the current bank. Borrowers having a good track record and have paid the instalments regularly are considered for transfer. Top up facility is also provided by banks simultaneously with transfer.

c – **Loan against Property (LAP) –** Home loans are typically provided for the purpose of construction or purchase of house/flat. However, if you own a property without any existing loan, and you need funds for any personal reasons, banks offer loans against property (LAP). These loans are offered with the interest rates in the range of 8-12%. The tenure of the loan can be up to 15 years.

d – **Reverse Mortgage Loan (RML) –** This loan is specially designed for people who are above 60 years of age and *do not* have a regular source of income. The loan is offered for the purpose of providing financial assistance to senior citizens who own a house. In a regular home loan, bank gives the loan and you pay the EMIs, whereas in reverse mortgage loan, bank mortgage the property and gives you money. The money you get is in two forms: some amount is given as lump-sum, whereas the remaining amount is given as monthly pension for a lifetime.

One major feature of this loan is that, there is no compulsion to pay the EMIs. The loan can be taken in the name of property holder alone or jointly with their spouse. Bank recovers the loan amount by selling the property after the death of borrower(s). The legal heirs of the borrower are given the option to repay the loan before the property is sold.

This loan is ideal for people who do not have regular source of income and do not wish to sell their property. The rate of interest on the loan varies between 9-12% and the tenure can be up to 20 years or more depending on the age of the borrower.

We have seen different types of home loan products. Borrowers can choose the products as per their needs and suitability. Apart from this, there are various other features in home loan

i – Banks give a concession of 0.05% in interest rates to women borrowers.

ii – If you have purchased a property but did not take the loan at that time, you can still avail the loan within a certain time period (usually 1 year). This is known as a home loan for reimbursement.

iii – Home loans can be availed in the form of Overdraft also (as discussed in loan against deposit). You have the option to convert your regular home loan into an overdraft facility even after taking the loan.

iv – Since 2019, the interest rates of home loans are determined by a system called EBLR. This rate is linked to RBI's lending rate. As a result, whenever RBI increases or decreases their rates, the interest rates on home loan also change accordingly. If you have already availed a loan before 2019 in previous system, you can convert it to current interest rate system. This facility is known as switch over. Banks charge a nominal fee for such conversions, but you can get the advantage of lower interest rates.

v – Banks conduct a legal scrutiny of property documents while giving home loan. This is done to ensure that there are no disputes or litigations related to the property. The documents are checked to verify their authenticity and to establish clear ownership of the property. This process is carried out to prevent the frauds. So, as a borrower, it protects you from future legal troubles. It is advised to carry out such legal scrutiny even if you are not availing loan, so that you can choose a dispute-free property.

The Government of India has launched a subsidy scheme for urban home loan borrowers by the name **Pradhan Mantri Awas Yojana (PMAY).** The scheme is for the borrowers who do not have an existing house in their name and purchasing the house first time with the help of a loan. The subsidy amount is deposited in the loan account which in turn reduces your EMI amount. The subsidy is divided into 4 income groups namely: Economically Weaker Section (EWS), Light Income Group (LIG), Medium Income Group (MIG 1) and MIG 2. The detailed chart of the scheme is as follows

CRITERIA	EWS	LIG	MIG 1	MIG 2
annual family income (In Rupees)	Upto 3 lakhs	Upto 6 lakhs	above 6 lakhs up to 12 lakhs	above 12 lakhs up to 18 lakhs
maximum carpet area of house	30 sq. mtr.*	60 sq. mtr.*	160 sq. mtr.	200 sq. mtr.
woman ownership in house required	yes #	yes #	Not mandatory	Not mandator y
maximum subsidy amount payable	Rs. 2.67 lakhs	Rs. 2.67 lakhs	Rs. 2.35 lakhs	Rs. 2.30 lakhs

*Bigger carpet area can be permitted in case of construction or purchase of house/flat to EWS and LIG. No relaxation is permitted for MIG1 and MIG2 borrowers.

Woman ownership (sole or co-owner) is waived in case of construction of a house on existing plot. But if purchasing the new property then woman co-ownership is mandatory to avail the subsidy for EWS and LIG group.

For the purpose of subsidy, the family is defined as husband, wife and unmarried children. No member in the family should own an existing house. The scheme has been discontinued since 31.03.2022, but according to some news reports, government is planning to re-introduce the scheme. The scheme is applicable to selected cities of India, and you can find more details and check your eligibility for the subsidy from the government's website https://pmayuclap.gov.in .

Though we have covered the basic points of home loans, there remains one important question to be answered: Whether to buy home? If yes, when is the best time to buy it? People nowadays are divided into two groups. Some suggest that it is better to live in a rented house whereas others argue that it is better to buy a house. Let us understand the logic behind their contrasting views.

Those who prefer renting a house give the following points in favor of their view:

i- Freedom to move- You can relocate to any place for better job opportunities or for various other reasons.

ii- Investment- Instead of paying an EMI for a house, you can invest that amount and create a corpus for your future. Additionally, when purchasing a house, you need to make a down payment, which can also be invested.

iii- Furniture and other cost- When you buy a house, there is a sizable cost associated with it such as stamp duty, furniture, property taxes, maintenance, repair/ renovations cost etc. You can save all these costs by renting a house.

iv- **Tax Benefit**- The monthly rent you pay can give you tax benefits under income tax.

v- Debt Free – You can live a debt-free life which also helps you to take certain decisions in life. Many people feel tied to their jobs because they have taken a home loan and cannot leave the job to do things of their choice due to these liabilities. Renting a house gives you the freedom of living the life on your terms.

Those who are in favor of buying a house give the following reasons to support their decision:

i- Emotional Comfort – Owning a house gives an emotional comfort of getting settled, to you and your family. It brings stability to the family.

ii- Landlord issues – There are numerous instances where landlords creates inconvenience to their tenants. You are not allowed to modify the home according to your preference. Plus there is always a problem of rent hike and eviction. Such issues are avoided by owning a house.

iii- Asset Creation – Buying a house creates an asset for future, which increases your net worth. Such assets can be passed on to your future generations.

iv- Tax Benefit – The EMI you pay is exempted from tax up to a certain limit which can reduce your tax liability.

v- Source of income – If for some reason you are not residing in the house you own, you can give it on rent which can become another source of income.

We have seen both sides of the argument and each side presents convincing points to support their opinion. Now let's try to find a middle ground that can help you to make a better decision.

i - EMI amount- It is advised to take a loan where the EMI amount does not exceed 40% of your net monthly income (NMI), so that remaining 60% can be utilized for monthly expenses and investment.

For example, if a person is having monthly salary of Rs. 30000, then banks may offer an option to deduct EMI up to 55% of the salary, which means your EMI amount will be Rs. 16500. Though it helps you to take higher loan amount but it will become difficult to manage the monthly expenses in remaining salary of Rs. 13500. If you cannot afford a good house in 40% EMI, it is advised to wait until your income increases, otherwise a higher EMI amount may lead to financial distress. It is better live stress-free in rented house than to be stressed in your own house.

ii- Down payment- As we discussed earlier in LTV ratio, banks do not provide 100% loan of the property value. Therefore, you have to pay the remaining amount as down payment. Along with this, there are other expenses such as stamp duty, taxes, insurance, and furniture cost. Sometimes, people take personal loan or other such loans to fund these costs which add to their monthly liability. It is important to avoid such mistakes when buying a home. You should consider buying a home when you have saved enough to bear these costs.

iii- Career priorities - If you wish to change your profession in the coming future from say job to a businessman, then buying a house can become a burden while switching. It is advisable to purchase a home only when you have fully decided on your career path.

iv- Tenure – Banks offer the option of loan tenure up to a maximum of 30 years, depending on your age. While many people advise keeping the loan tenure short so that you pay less interest but in my opinion, having a loan for a longer tenure is beneficial for the following reasons.

a-No foreclosure/prepayment charges – Banks usually do not charge foreclosure/prepayment charges on home loan. So even if you take loan for a longer period, you always have the option to close the loan as per your choice.

b- Ease of availing other loan – As we discussed earlier, you can avail top up loan on your home loan. Suppose you have taken a home loan for 15 years and then apply for a top up loan after 5 years.

Some banks may offer you a tenure of only 10 years for the top-up loan since the remaining tenure of the home loan is 10 years. This can increase the monthly EMI burden and may also reduce your loan eligibility as per EMI/NMI ratio. To avoid such situations, it is suggested to have longer tenure for your home loans.

c- Tax benefit- With a longer tenure, you can enjoy tax benefits for a longer period. People usually close their home loan upon retirement, but some people receive pension which is also taxable. In such cases, a home loan can help to save your taxes to a great extent.

d - Reduced EMI – With longer tenures, your EMI amount gets reduced which helps you to spend your remaining salary on other expenses. With shorter tenures, the EMI amount is higher, and in the event of any financial emergency it can become difficult to allocate funds accordingly. In such cases, you can miss out on your EMIs which may hamper your credit history.

The reduced EMI also gives you the option of investing the remaining amount, which can help you create a corpus for future. Let's understand this with the following images.

Image 2

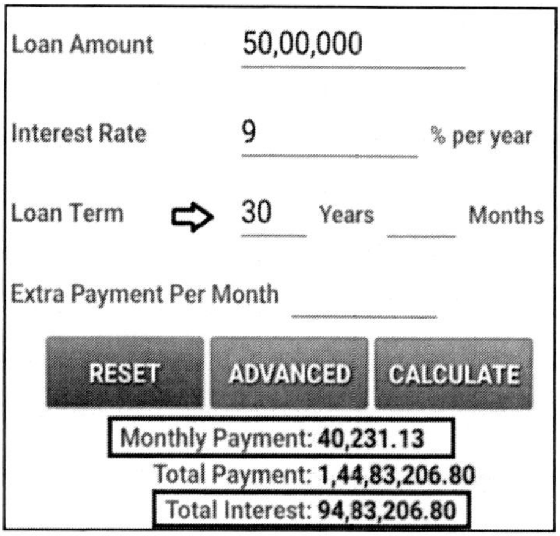

Image 3

As you can see in images, a loan is availed of Rs. 50,00,000 for 20 years and 30 years. The EMI for 20 years is Rs. 44,986 whereas for 30 years is Rs. 40,231. There is a difference of Rs. 4755 between the two EMIs.

At the beginning of this chapter, we have taken the example of Vivek and Nilesh. The trick Vivek used was that, he took the loan for a longer tenure and invested the difference amount. Considering that he invested in instruments which gave him returns at 12%, the result is as follows:

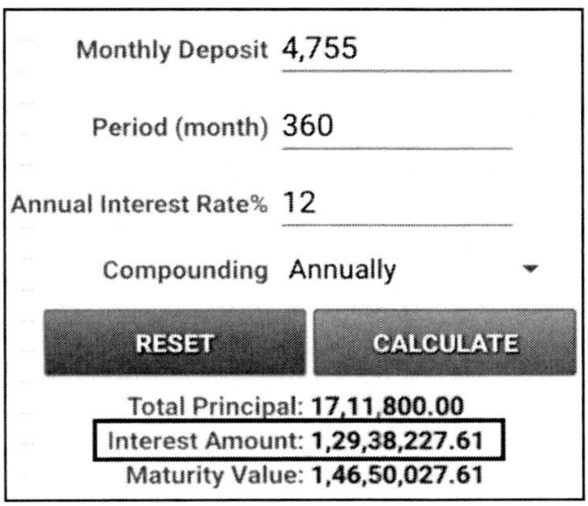

Image 4

As you can compare in image 3 and image 4, Vivek has paid a total interest of Rs. 94.83 lakhs on his loan, while he has received an interest of Rs. 1.29 crores. This effectively makes his loan a zero-interest loan.

Basically, Vivek has used the magic of compounding in investing to tackle the effects of compounding in loan making him a *successful compounder!!!.* Since you are now well informed about the different products of investments and loans, you can also create such tricks to achieve your financial goals. The following points should be remembered while taking a loan.

i- Various features of loan, such as tenure, rate of interest, margin, processing fees may vary from bank to bank. You should always check and compare these factors before availing a loan. Eligibility criteria also differ among banks, so if you are not eligible at one particular bank, then you should explore options with other banks.

ii- There are various offers on loan during festive season (typically from August till December) such as discounts on interest rates, processing fees waiver, etc. You can take advantage of these offers, if you plan to take the loan during festive periods.

iii- Banks nowadays are doing tie up with various companies and govt. departments to open salary accounts of their employees. If your salary account is opened under such salary package tie-up, then there are various benefits in loans provided by banks. You can check for such benefits from the bank's official website.

iv- While signing the loan documents, read all the terms and conditions carefully. All the information which was provided to you should be reflected in those documents. If there is a mismatch, you can ask the bank officials to correct the same. If you do not understand any part of those documents, you can ask the bank officials to explain the same to you.

v- When you avail a loan, you should ask for a copy of "terms and conditions" letter. It is mandatory for banks to provide you with such a letter. All the information regarding the loan is mentioned in that letter. Such letters are also called arrangement letter. If you have already availed a loan and did not take a copy, you can ask for the same, from your bank branch anytime during the loan.

vi- When you repay and close the loan, always ask for a "No Dues Certificate" from the bank. This certificate can be used for various purposes in future and it also confirms the clearance of all dues related to the loan.

Here we have finished the chapter. Hope this chapter will help you to select the correct loans according to your needs. We will now proceed to our next chapter.

CHAPTER 4
BUSINESS LOANS

Mrs. Sneha is a housewife living in a semi-urban city. She has a keen interest in the preparation of home-made spices and she also distributes the same to her neighbours. Looking at the quality of the spices, one of her neighbours suggested that she should consider starting a business of spices. Fascinated by the idea, Mrs. Sneha discussed it with her husband, and both of them visited the bank to enquire about a business loan. They met branch manager Mr. Manoj, and shared their business idea. Upon hearing their plan, Mr. Manoj suggested some loan schemes that could help them set-up the business. Let us find out about those schemes in this chapter.

All the loan products we discussed in the previous chapter are called personal-segment loans. However, in addition to these, banks also provide loans for the purpose of setting up a new business or expanding an existing business. The Government of India also introduces schemes to help new businesses by providing various subsidies. These loans are categorized into the following types:

1- Agriculture Loans

2-MSME (Micro, Small& Medium Enterprises) Loans

Let's see in detail about both the types

AGRICULTURE LOANS

More than 50% of the Indian population is engaged in agriculture, making it the largest employment-generating sector in India. Agriculture loans are provided to meet the financial needs of the farming. These loans are given in the following ways:

a- **Kisan Credit Card (KCC)** – These loans are given for fulfilling the expenses related to cultivation of crops which includes purchasing seeds, fertilizers, and other such expenses. India has two crop seasons, namely Kharif (monsoon season) and Rabi season (winter). These crops are called short-term crops, and there are also some long-term crops such as mango, coconuts and more. KCC loan can be availed for the cultivation of both types of crops.

These loans are to be repaid after the harvesting season is over. KCC loans up to Rs. 3 lakhs are given at the interest rate of 7%, and the prompt-paying borrowers are given an interest subvention of 3% from the government. So, if the farmer repays the crop loan on time, the effective interest rate comes down to only 4%. Due to all these features, KCC becomes an excellent choice to raise funds for farming.

b- **Agriculture Term Loans (ATL)** – Apart from the cultivation of crops, there are various agriculture-related expenses. ATLs are provided to fulfil these expenses. These loans are usually provided for the following purposes:

i- Purchase of farm machinery such as power tiller, harvester etc.

ii- Construction of a compound wall.

ii- Minor irrigation facilities which includes digging of well/ ponds, bore well, tube well, sprinkler, drip irrigation, purchase of pump sets.

iv- Purchase of tractors

v- Purchase of livestock such as cows and buffaloes, as well as for the purpose of fisheries, beekeeping, poultry, goat farming, etc.

These loans have tenure of 5 years or more and the interest rate ranges between 10-12%. ATLs can be availed from any bank in India. A specialized bank is also set up for the purpose of agriculture and rural development in India by the name of NABARD (National Bank for Agriculture and Rural Development). In addition to the purposes mentioned above, there are various specialized agriculture-related businesses that are covered under ATL. The list of such businesses can be accessed from the NABARD website https://nabard.org.

MSME LOANS

Apart from agriculture, businesses can be broadly classified into the following three sectors:

i- Manufacturing Sector – Any business that converts raw materials into finished products comes under the manufacturing sector. For example, factories that produce cars are part of the manufacturing sector.

ii- Trading Sector- Any business that acts as an intermediary between manufacturers and consumers comes under the trading sector. For example, showrooms selling cars to customers are part of the trading sector.

iii- Service Sector – Any business that provides services comes under the service sector. For example, servicing centres that repair cars are part of the service sector.

Individuals can start their business in any of the sectors mentioned above. Banks provide business loans to new businesses as well as already-established businesses. The Government of India also supports businessmen by introducing various schemes. We will see some of the prominent schemes which can help entrepreneurs to start their businesses.

1) **Mudra Loan** - Launched in 2015 by Govt. of India, Mudra loans are given to businessmen to support them in establishing or expanding their businesses. The maximum loan amount that can be availed under the Mudra scheme is capped at Rs. 10 lakhs. The loans are given for a period of 5 years, and the rate of interest for the loan is usually around 12%. These loans can be availed for any purpose such as manufacturing, trading or the service sector business.

As we discussed in home loans, the house is taken as collateral which acts as a security for the loan. If the borrower fails to repay the loan, banks have the option to sell the house to recover the loan amount. However, in the case of Mudra loans, no such collateral is required to avail the loan.

Now, you must be wondering how the bank will recover the loan in case the borrower fails to repay the loan. For this, we will now try to understand the concept of a "credit guarantee."

Since, it is not possible for everyone to provide collateral for business loans, the Government of India acts as a guarantor for such loans. To enable this, the government has established a guarantee fund called the "Credit Guarantee Fund for Micro Units" (CGFMU). The loans given under the Mudra scheme are covered by this fund. Therefore, if a borrower fails to repay the loan, the banks can claim the unpaid loan amount from the government.

To avail the facility of credit guarantee, the borrower is required to pay an annual guarantee fee (AGF) to cover the loan under CGFMU. The fee is usually 1% of the loan amount. For instance, if you have availed a loan of Rs. 5 lakhs, an annual fee of 1% which is Rs. 5000 will have to be paid to avail the collateral-free Mudra loan. This fee must be paid every year till the loan is fully repaid. In subsequent years, the fee is charged on the outstanding loan amount. So, if you have availed a loan of Rs. 5 lakhs which reduces to Rs. 4 lakhs in the second year, the fee amount will also reduce to Rs. 4000 and so on. The details regarding CGFMU can be accessed from the portal https://www.ncgtc.in.

Mudra loan can be availed from any bank in India, and detailed information regarding the products of the loan is available at https://www.mudra.org.in .

2) **Prime Minister's Employment Generation Programme (PMEGP)** – As the name suggests, the objective of the PMEGP scheme is to generate employment opportunities in both rural and urban areas of the country. The maximum loan amount that can be availed under PMEGP is capped at Rs. 50 lakhs. The loan can be availed by any individual above 18 years of age, having a minimum educational qualification of 8th standard. However, it is to be noted that only new projects are considered for approval under the PMEPG loan scheme.

To help with the process of PMEGP, the government has established a "District Industries Centre" (DIC) in every district of the country. Applicants can visit the DIC office in their respective districts to get detailed information about all the government schemes, including PMEGP, and submit their loan applications. These loan applications are then forwarded to banks for review and sanction, along with necessary documents.

In addition to DIC, the government has also established training centres in each district to provide training regarding business. These training institutes are known as "Rural Self Employment Training Institutes" (RSETI). Applicants are required to complete the training to avail the loan under PMEGP.

Just like the Mudra loan, the PMEGP loan can also be availed with the help of a credit guarantee. Here, the credit guarantee is given by another fund called "Credit Guarantee Trust fund for Micro and

Small Enterprises" (CGTMSE). The annual guarantee fee (AGF) is charged in the range of 0.50- 1% of the loan amount. However, for those having collateral security, they can avoid paying the guarantee fee by providing collateral (plot, house etc.) to the bank.

In addition to this, borrowers can also get the benefit of subsidy if they pay their loan regularly. The subsidy ranges between 10- 35% of the loan amount. For example, if a person has availed a loan of Rs. 50 lakhs and the subsidy is 20%, they will receive Rs. 10 lakhs as subsidy, and they will be required to repay the remaining 40 lakhs with interest.

All business loans are given either as a term loan (TL) or as cash credit (CC). The term loan is given for the purpose where the expenses are permanent in nature, such as the construction of factory, purchase of machinery etc. On the other hand, the cash credit is provided to meet the daily requirements of business, such as purchasing raw material, bill payments etc. Cash credit is similar to an overdraft account which we have discussed in the previous chapter. Some businesses has both types of expenses, so they can avail term loan and cash credit together, such loan is called as composite loan.

I guess you might have been overwhelmed by all these concepts. To make these concepts more relatable, let's consider the example of Mrs. Sneha, which we discussed earlier in this chapter. She decides to establish her spice business and considers availing a loan under the PMEGP scheme. She visits the DIC office located in her district to learn more about the scheme and gather the necessary information. The DIC officer explains the scheme to her and provides a list of documents required for loan application.

Mrs. Sneha then calculates the expenses for setting up her business. The spice business requires raw materials such as raw spices (turmeric, chilli, garlic, coriander etc.), packaging materials and other costs such as factory rent, electricity rent, and labour salary. Along with this, some machines are also required for grinding, processing and packing the spices. After considering all the costs, she decides to apply for a loan of Rs. 40 lakhs. Out of this amount, Rs, 25 lakhs will be used for utilized for purchasing machinery (term loan), while the remaining Rs. 15 lakhs will be utilized for raw materials and other daily requirements (cash credit).

She then submits all the required documents to the DIC office and applies for the loan. The DIC office then forwards her application and documents to the bank for loan sanctioning process. After the loan is sanctioned, the bank asks her to complete the mandatory training at the local RSETI. The training certificate is to be submitted to the bank after which the bank disburses the loan amount. Bank then gives her a specific time period (moratorium period) of say 3-6 months to set up her business. After her unit starts functioning, she starts paying the EMI. If she pays her loan regularly, the government will release the subsidy amount. Assuming that the subsidy is 35%, in which case Mrs. Sneha would receive a subsidy of Rs. 14 lakhs. This subsidy amount is then deposited in her loan account, which means that her loan will be reduced to Rs. 26 lakhs only.

For existing well-performing units that have paid their first PMEGP loan on time, a second PMEGP loan can be availed to expand/upgrade their existing business. The subsidy in the second PMEGP loan is up to 20% of the loan amount. Due to all these benefits, PMEGP acts as a good option for people who want to start a new business. This loan can be availed from any bank in India, and the details of the scheme can be accessed from the portal https://kviconline.gov.in.

3) **Stand-Up India**- This loan scheme is launched by the government to promote entrepreneurship among Scheduled Castes (SC), Scheduled Tribes (ST) and women entrepreneurs, enabling them to start a new business. The minimum loan amount under the scheme is Rs. 10 lakhs, whereas the maximum loan amount is capped at Rs. 1 crore. The loan can be obtained for tenure of up to 7 years, and a credit guarantee scheme is also available. Stand-Up India loans

can be availed from any bank in India, and the details of the scheme can be accessed from the website https://www.standupmitra.in.

These were some of the prominent government schemes for business loans. Following points should be remembered while availing any business loan:

i- **Business Registration –** While starting any business, a registration certificate is to be obtained to legally conduct the business. This certificate is known by various names such as shop-act license, gumasta license or trade license. This license can be easily obtained online from the respective state government website. Additionally, the government has introduced Udyog Aadhar/ Udyam Certificate for business registration, which can also be obtained online from https://eudyogaadhaar.org. Both these certificates can be used for opening a bank account and to avail a loan. Therefore, it is advised to obtain these certificates before commencing the business.

ii- Project Report – While applying for a business loan, a project report of the business needs to be submitted to the bank.

A project report is a document which contains information such as introduction of the business, business goals, budget, market potential and profitability of the business. Banks evaluate these reports before approving the loan, which makes it a crucial document for any business loan. So it is recommended to prepare a comprehensive project report that represents accurate picture of the business. These reports can also be prepared with the help of professionals such as Chartered Accountants (C.A.).

iii- Margin Money – Banks generally do not provide 100% of the finance required to start a business. Some amount has to be invested by the applicant which is called as margin money. Usually, the margin money is in the range of 10-25% of the finance required. It is advised to check the margin money requirement with the bank before applying for a loan.

iv- Schemes – The government offers various schemes to support entrepreneurs establishing their business. Both the central government and state government run such schemes. Details of these schemes can be obtained from the local DIC office or from the MSME portal https://msme.gov.in. Applicants can also inquire at the bank for information on these schemes, enabling them to apply for the most suitable scheme according to their requirements.

With this, we have completed the chapter on business loans. Now, let's move on to the next chapter.

CHAPTER 5
TAXATION

Mr. Ashish is a senior employee working in a multinational company with an annual income of Rs. 10,00,000 . He has a family consisting of his wife and two children. His wife is a homemaker, and one of his children is pursuing graduation, while the other child is in 10th standard. Despite earning a good salary, Mr. Ashish does not have to pay any income tax. In this chapter, we will explore how he manages to save on his taxes.

Many people fear when they hear the word tax. Everyone wants to earn money but rarely do people want to pay taxes on it. However, tax is a necessary part of a functioning society, and every good citizen should pay the tax. It helps building the nation and enables the government to carry out various schemes for its citizens. The government also helps you to save taxes by giving various rebates. Tax rates are divided into different slabs based on your gross annual income, which are as follows

Annual Income	Tax Rate
Up to Rs. 2.5 lakhs	Nil
Rs. 2.5 lakhs to Rs. 5 lakhs	5%
Rs. 5 lakhs to Rs. 10 lakhs	20%
Rs. 10 lakhs and above	30%

Image 1

As per the chart above, Mr. Ashish falls into the 30% tax slab. Now, let's explore the various sections available in Income Tax Act that enables us to take the rebate.

1-**Section 80C-** This section allows a tax deduction of up to Rs. 1.50 lakhs on your investments. These investments include PPF, SSA, NSC, life insurance premiums, 5 years FDs, ELSS. If you have purchased a home, the cost of stamp duty and registration charges can be included for tax deduction in that year. Additionally, if you have availed home loan for purchasing the property, the principal amount paid towards the loan every year is also included in this section. Tuition fees paid for up to 2 children in a year can also be included for tax exemption. Within 80C, there are two sub-sections that cover the contribution to the National Pension System (NPS).

i) Section 80CCD (1): This allows a tax deduction of 10% of annual salary within the ceiling of Rs. 1.50 lakhs towards NPS contributions. This section falls under the overall ceiling of Section 80C. Therefore, you can claim a maximum tax deduction of Rs. 1.50 lakhs by using either Section 80C or Section 80CCD (1), or both of them combined.

ii)Section 80CCD(1B): This section provides an additional tax deduction of Rs. 50,000 over and above the ceiling of Rs. 1.50 lakhs towards NPS contribution. If you have already availed tax benefit of Rs. 1.50 lakhs under the above sections, you can avail additional tax benefit of Rs. 50,000 under this section.

By utilizing above three sections, you can claim a maximum tax deduction of Rs. 2 lakhs, which means, it reduces your taxable income, which in turn reduces your tax liability. For example, if your annual income is Rs. 8 lakhs, and you make investments under these sections, then you will only have to pay tax on Rs. 6 lakhs.

2- **Section 80D** – This section provides a tax deduction for the amount of premium you pay for **medical insurance**, up to Rs. 25000 per year. The insurance can be obtained for self, spouse and dependent children. You can claim an additional Rs. 5000 per year for preventive health check-up for yourself and family. If you have purchased medical insurance for your parents, you can claim a deduction of up to Rs. 50,000 in your income tax. So the maximum deduction that can be claimed under section 80D is up to Rs. 80,000.

There is another section called **80DDB** which is specifically for **medical expenditure**. If you have incurred the cost of medical treatment for yourself or dependent family members, you can claim a deduction from your taxable income under this section. An amount up to Rs. 40,000 can be claimed for medical expenditure. If you have a medical insurance policy and some payment is received from the insurance company for medical expenses, then that amount needs to be subtracted from the allowable deduction amount. For example, if you have received say Rs. 25,000 from the insurance company, then you can claim the remaining Rs. 15,000 as deduction under this section.

Under this section, the limit for tax deduction for medical expenditure incurred for a senior citizen (above 60 years of age) is Rs. 1 lakh. This means that if you have incurred medical expenses for a senior citizen, you can claim a deduction of up to Rs. 1 lakh from your taxable income. There is a list of specified diseases covered under this section. The list of such diseases can be obtained from income tax department website https://incometaxindia.gov.in .

3- **Section 80E –** This section deals with the **interest on education loans**. If you have taken an education loan for yourself or dependent family members, the interest paid on the loan for the first 8 years (during repayment) can be claimed for tax deduction. There is no upper limit for the deduction, and you can claim the total interest paid for tax deduction.

4- **Section 24 (b) –** This section is related to a tax deduction on **home loan interest**. If you have purchased a house through a loan, you can deduct the interest amount up to Rs. 2 lakhs per year from your taxable income. As we have discussed in section 80C, you can claim a tax deduction up to Rs. 1.50 lakhs on the principal amount of the home loan. In section 24 (b), you can claim tax deduction of up to Rs. 2 lakhs on the home loan interest. Therefore, the total tax deduction that can be claimed on a home loan is up to Rs. 3.50 lakhs.

If you purchase the house jointly with a family member and both of you are earning, then both individuals can claim separate tax deduction of up to Rs. 3.50 lakhs each. This means the total tax deduction can be up to Rs. 7 lakhs per year.

5- **Section 80GG -** This section deals with the deduction for **house rent paid** by an individual. If you are a salaried employee and do not receive house rent allowance (HRA) from your company, or if you are a businessman/self-employed individual staying at a rented house, you can claim this tax deduction. The total amount of tax deduction is the least of the following three:

i – Amount of Rs. 5,000 per month (Rs. 60,000 per year)

ii – Yearly rent minus 10% of annual income

iii – 25% of the total annual income

Let's assume your annual income is Rs. 12 lakhs and the monthly rent you pay is Rs. 20000 (yearly rent Rs.2,40,000). Then the tax deduction will be calculated as follows:

Condition	Rule	Amount
1	60000 per year	60000
2	Yearly rent - 10% of annual income	240000 - 120000 =120000
3	25% of annual income	300000

Image 2

So as per the above chart, the least amount is Rs. 60000, which you can claim for tax deduction under section 80GG. One important condition regarding this section is that: you, your spouse or your minor children should not own a house anywhere in India.

6 – **Standard Deduction -** This provision is for salaried employees having annual income above Rs. 5 lakhs. According to this provision, you can claim a **standard deduction of Rs. 50,000** on your taxable income. For example, if your annual income is Rs. 10 lakhs, then you would only have to pay tax on Rs. 9.50 lakhs.

We have taken the example of Mr. Ashish at the beginning of this chapter. He is earning Rs. 10 lakhs per year and considering that he has done the following investments, let's see how much tax he can save. Please note that all the values taken here are for the purpose of understanding only. The values may vary from person to person.

Section	Product	Amount invested / paid	Tax deduction received
80C	Any product or combination of products under 80C	1.50 lakhs	1.50 lakhs
80CCD(1B)	NPS	0.60 lakhs	0.50 lakhs
80D	Medical insurance for family and parents	0.50 lakhs	0.50 lakhs

80E	Education Loan interest for children	0.50 lakhs	0.50 lakhs
Sec. 24	Home loan interest	1.50 lakhs	1.50 lakhs
Std. deduction	Salaried employee	0	0.50 lakhs
		Total tax deduction received	5 lakhs

Image 3

The taxable income of Mr. Ashish is now reduced to Rs. 5 lakhs as he has saved tax on Rs. 5 lakhs by using the above sections. Referring to image 1 of this chapter, we can see that there is no tax on income up to Rs. 2.50 lakhs, and a 5% tax on the next 2.50 lakhs. Therefore, he has to pay a tax of Rs. 12,500. However, according to income tax rules, if your total taxable income is up to Rs. 5 lakhs, you can claim a tax rebate of Rs.12,500 by filling the Income Tax Return (ITR). This rebate is provided under **Section 87A** of the income tax act. Hence, by filing the ITR, Mr. Ashish can take a rebate of Rs. 12500, making his taxes practically zero.

Now let us see if Mr. Ashish had not used any of the sections discussed earlier, how much tax he will have to pay?

Income	Amount	Tax Rate	Tax amount
Up to Rs. 2.5 lakhs	2.50 lakhs	Nil	Nil
Rs. 2.5 lakhs to Rs. 5 lakhs	2.50 lakhs	5%	12,500
Rs. 5 lakhs to Rs. 9.5 lakhs	4.50 lakhs	20%	90,000
		Total Tax	1,02,500

Image 4

As you can see, a substantial amount of tax can be saved by using these sections. Apart from the sections listed above, there are several other sections which can be used by taxpayers to reduce their taxes. Opinions from the tax advisor should be taken for such deductions while filling ITR.

The above mentioned taxation method corresponds to the old tax regime. The government of India has introduced a new tax regime in the year 2020. Taxpayers can opt for any of the tax regime as per their choice. The tax slabs in new tax regime are as follows:

Annual Income	**Tax Rate**
Up to Rs. 3 lakhs	Nil
Rs. 3 lakhs to Rs. 6 lakhs	5%
Rs. 6 lakhs to Rs. 9 lakhs	10%
Rs. 9 lakhs to Rs. 12 lakhs	15%
Rs. 12 lakhs to Rs. 15 lakhs	20%
Above Rs. 15 lakhs	30%

Image 5

The main difference between old and new tax regime is that, under the new tax regime, you cannot avail the deductions under any of the sections we have discussed earlier. Only a standard deduction of Rs. 50,000 can be claimed in new tax regime. However, the limit for section 87A is increased to Rs. 25,000 in new tax regime whereas it remains at Rs. 12,500 in old tax regime.

To understand it further, let's consider the case of Mr. Ashish, who has an annual income of Rs. 10 lakhs. By applying the standard deduction of Rs. 50,000 available to salaried employees, his taxable income would now be Rs. 9.50 lakhs Let's see how much tax he has to pay under new tax regime.

Annual Income	Amount	Tax Rate	Tax Amount
Up to Rs. 3 lakhs	Rs. 3 lakhs	Nil	Nil
Rs. 3 lakhs to Rs. 6 lakhs	Rs. 3 lakhs	5%	15,000
Rs. 6 lakhs to Rs. 9 lakhs	Rs. 3 lakhs	10%	30,000
Rs. 9 lakhs to Rs. 9.5 lakhs	Rs. 0.50 lakhs	15%	7500
		Total Tax	52,500

Image 6

If we compare image 4 and image 6, it becomes clear that new tax regime is beneficial for those who have do not made any investments or availed any loans. However, if we compare image 3 and image 6, it is evident that old tax regime can help you to save a significant amount of taxes. You can choose old or new tax regime, depending on your investments and loans.

As we have seen in old tax regime, the income up to Rs. 5 lakhs is can be exempted from tax, whereas in new tax regime the income up to Rs. 7.50 lakhs can be exempted from tax. Let's see how that works.

If your annual income is Rs. 7.50 lakhs, you can take a standard deduction of Rs. 50,000 which makes your taxable income to Rs. 7 lakhs. Now applying the brackets of new tax regime, the tax payable will be as follows.

Annual Income	Amount	Tax Rate	Tax Amount
Up to Rs. 3 lakhs	Rs. 3 lakhs	Nil	Nil
Rs. 3 lakhs to Rs. 6 lakhs	Rs. 3 lakhs	5%	15,000
Rs. 6 lakhs to Rs. 7 lakhs	Rs. 1 lakh	10%	10,000
		Total Tax	25,000

Image 7

The total tax liability is now Rs. 25,000. However, as per the new tax regime, if the total taxable income is up to Rs. 7 lakhs, you can claim tax rebate of Rs. 25,000 by filling the income tax return. This rebate is provided under section 87A of the income tax act. Taxpayers have the option of choosing any of the tax regimes as per their convenience and benefit. A tax advisor should be consulted for taking an informed decision which can help you save maximum tax.

Apart from the tax on salary/business income, there are additional sources of income that are also subject to tax. We have discussed various investment products in chapter 2. The interest or income you earn from the investments is called other income, which is added to your regular salary/business income for the purpose of calculating the tax. Other income usually includes the following:

i) Interest received from investments

ii) Rent income from property

iii) Gain from the sale of assets such as house, plot etc.

iv) Profit or gain received from the share market, mutual funds, and other investments.

The other income earned from all such sources needs to be considered for taxation in every financial year. Let us understand this with the help of an example.

Mr. Ashish has an annual income of Rs. 10 lakhs from his salary. Additionally, he has invested Rs. 5 lakhs in a fixed deposit for duration of 3 years. Assuming that the interest earned in the first year is Rs. 25000, his total annual income will become Rs. 10.25 lakhs. Even though Mr. Ashish will receive the total interest amount after 3 years, the interest accrued every year will be treated as income for taxation. Now we will see how the tax is applied on investments.

a- **Fixed Deposit & MOD** – The interest received on FD/MOD is not taxable if the interest amount is less than Rs. 10,000 in a financial year.

If the annual income of a depositor is less than taxable income, then the interest received on FD will not be taxable. For example, if your annual income is Rs. 2 lakhs and the interest received on FD is Rs. 50,000 in a year, then you do not need to pay tax as the total income is Rs. 2.50 lakhs which is not taxable as per income tax rules. In such situations, you need to fill out a form called 15G/15H in the bank while creating FD.

If your annual income is taxable and the total interest received on your FD is more than Rs. 10,000, you have to pay tax as per your applicable tax slab.

b- **PPF & SSA**- As we discussed earlier, the amount you invest in PPF up to Rs. 1.50 lakhs can be deducted from tax under Section 80C. The interest received on maturity is also non-taxable. Therefore, the total corpus you receive is tax-free. Since the principal, interest and maturity amount are exempted from tax, such instruments are called Exempt-Exempt-Exempt (EEE**).** Similar to PPF, the Sukanya Samriddhi Account also falls under EEE category.

c- **NPS** – The tier-1 account of NPS falls under EEE category as the investment and interest received at maturity is tax-free. However, the pension amount you receive will be taxable if your annual pension income falls within taxable bracket. There are no tax benefits for tier-2 account.

d- **KVP** – The amount invested in KVP is not eligible for tax deduction tax under 80C, and the returns received on maturity are also taxable according to your tax slab.

e- **NSC** – This product is partially taxable as the amount invested by depositor can be deducted from tax under Section 80C. However, the interest amount received in the final year is taxable as per the tax slab of depositor.

f – **Government Bond** – The interest received on the bonds is considered as other income and will be taxed as per the tax slab of bond holder.

Except for NPS, all the investments mentioned above are fixed interest investments. There are other products, such as shares, SGB, etc. where the profit from investment depends on the increasing price of the product. The profit you receive from these products is called capital gains, and the tax paid on it is known as capital gains tax. Depending on the duration of the profit, these capital gains are divided into two categories: short-term capital gain (STCG) and long-term capital gain (LTCG).

When it comes to capital gains, you can get advantage of indexation. As inflation rises, the prices of commodities increase. To adjust the tax in accordance with inflation, the government announces cost inflation index (CII) rates every year. The list for such index values is as follows:

Financial Year	Cost Inflation Index (CII)	Financial Year	Cost Inflation Index (CII)
2001-02	100	2012-13	200
2002-03	105	2013-14	220
2003-04	109	2014-15	240
2004-05	113	2015-16	254
2005-06	117	2016-17	264
2006-07	122	2017-18	272
2007-08	129	2018-19	280
2008-09	137	2019-20	289
2009-10	148	2020-21	301
2010-11	167	2021-22	317
2011-12	184	2022-23	331

Image 8

Let's understand the concept of indexation and how it helps in saving capital gains tax with the help of following example:

Mr. Ashish purchased a plot in April- 2001 for Rs. 5 lakhs. He sold the plot in April-2020 for Rs. 45 lakhs, making a profit of Rs. 40 lakhs. Assuming the capital gain tax was at 20% in that year, the total amount of tax would be 20% of Rs. 40 lakhs, which comes to Rs. 8 lakhs.

However, since the inflation has also increased during those years, indexation is applied to determine the adjusted purchase cost of the property. The formula for indexation is as follows:

$$Indexation = \frac{C.I.I.\text{ in the selling year}}{C.I.I\text{ in the purchasing year}} * \text{Purchase cost}$$

Purchase cost being Rs. 5 lakhs and taking C.I.I. values from image 8, the adjusted purchase cost of the plot will be

$$\frac{\mathbf{301}}{\mathbf{100}} * 500000 = 1505000$$

With the adjusted cost is now calculated, the profit from the sale will be 45 lakhs minus15.05 lakhs, which amounts to is 29.95 lakhs. Now, the tax will be levied on revised profit of 29.95 lakhs at 20% which will be Rs. 5.99 lakhs. In this way, indexation has helped to reduce the tax from Rs. 8 lakhs to Rs. 5.99 lakhs. Now we will see how the taxes are levied on remaining products.

g- **SGB –** The interest received on Sovereign Gold Bond is taxed as per tax slab of SGB holder. If the SGB is sold before 3 years, it will be subject to STCG tax as per the applicable tax slab. If sold after 3 years, LTCG tax at 20% after indexation will be levied. You can calculate the indexation amount before paying tax using the method explained earlier.

The maturity period of SGB is 8 years, and no capital gain tax is levied if SGB is redeemed at its maturity.

h- **Corporate Bond & Debentures** – The interest received every year on bonds is taxed as per applicable tax slab of investor.

Bonds can be purchased directly when they are issued by the company. The company pays the interest until maturity, and the original investment is returned to the investor upon maturity. In such cases, there is no capital gain, and therefore no capital gains tax is applied.

Bonds can also be purchased from your demat account. If you sell your bonds at a higher price than your purchase price, capital gains tax is to be paid on such profits. If bonds are sold before 3 years, they are subject STCG tax as per the tax slab of bondholder. If sold after 3 years, they are subject to LTCG tax at 20% after indexation. Debentures are also taxed in the same manner as bonds.

i- **Mutual Funds-** Mutual funds can be broadly categorized into two types: Equity Mutual Fund and Debt Mutual Funds. We will see how each of them is taxed.

-**Equity Mutual Fund –** If more than 65% of the fund's asset is invested in equity instruments such as shares etc, that mutual fund is considered as equity mutual fund. The period for STCG and LTCG is 1 year. So if mutual fund is redeemed /withdrawn before 1 year, short term capital gains tax is applied, whereas if done after 1 year then long term capital gains tax is applied. The STCG tax rate for equity mutual fund is 15% irrespective of your tax slab.

There is no LTCG tax on mutual funds up to Rs. 1 lakhs if withdrawn/ redeemed after 1 year. If the gain amount exceeds Rs. 1 lakh, then LTCG tax at 10% will be levied and no indexation benefit is provided for this tax.

To understand it better, let's consider that you have made a gain of Rs. 10 lakhs in equity mutual fund after a period of say 5 years. While withdrawing the amount, the amount of Rs.1 lakh will not be taxed, but the remaining amount of Rs.9 lakhs will be taxed at 10%, resulting in Rs. 90,000 in tax liability.

-**Debt Mutual Fund-** If more than 65% of the fund's asset is invested in debt instruments like bonds, debentures etc, that mutual fund is considered as debt mutual fund. There is no provision of STCG and LTCG in debt mutual fund, so the profit made on debt mutual fund will be taxed as per your tax slab. For example, if you make a profit of Rs. 2 lakhs and you fall into the 20% tax bracket, you will need to pay tax of Rs.40000 on the profit.

Another type of mutual fund we discussed in chapter 2 is ELSS. The amount invested in ELSS is locked in for a period of 3 years; therefore, only LTCG tax is applied, as per equity mutual funds.

Additionally, the amount invested in ELSS can be deducted from tax under Section 80C of the Income Tax Act.

j-**Share Market & Nifty BeES –** The profit received from shares and nifty bees are taxed in similar manner to equity mutual funds. The period for capital gain for shares/bees is 1 year. Shares sold before 1 year are subject to STCG tax of 15% irrespective of your tax slab. Shares sold after 1 year are subject to LTCG tax of 10% without indexation if the profit amount exceeds Rs. 1 lakh. In case you receive dividends on your shares, it will be treated as other income and will be taxed as per your tax slab.

k- **REIT –** The interest received on REIT is taxed as per tax slab of the investor. If any gains are made from investing in REIT, they will be taxed as per equity market rules discussed above.

l-**Crypto-currency-** All the investments we discussed earlier will be taxed only if there is a gain or income. For example, if you have purchased shares of 2 companies and made a profit of Rs. 5 lakhs from one company but incurred a loss of Rs. 1 lakh on another company, your total taxable profit will be considered as Rs. 4 lakhs, and you would need to pay tax on that amount. However, this adjustment facility is not available in crypto-currency. If any profit is made from crypto-currency, a flat tax rate of 30% will be levied on that profit but the loss will not be adjusted with the profit. No STCG, LTCG or indexation benefit is provided for crypto-currency tax.

The following points should be kept in mind while dealing with taxes.

i- Many individuals try to hide their income to avoid paying income tax. This practice should be avoided as it can invite legal troubles in the future. Additionally, it can also reduce the eligibility for any loan. Banks consider the income shown in the Income Tax Return (ITR) while giving loans, so showing less income in the ITR may hinder the chances of obtaining the required loan amount.

ii- For individuals who own agricultural land, they can include the income in their ITR. According to section 10(1), agriculture income earned in India is exempt from tax. Therefore, you can report agriculture income without paying any additional tax.

iii- It is important to file ITR on time to avoid late fees imposed by the government. Banks also prefer applicants who file their ITR promptly. People who file the ITRs irregularly are not considered for loans by some banks. Therefore, timely filing of the ITR is crucial to avoid future issues.

With this, we have completed our chapter on taxation. You can now make financial decisions based on their tax implications and plan your investments and loans accordingly. It is advised to consult your tax planner/advisor for further details. They will give you a detailed idea regarding the taxes and keep you informed about any modifications in tax rules by the government.

CHAPTER 6
INSURANCE

Prashant and Pravin are family friends residing in the same society. They planned a family vacation to Paris for duration of 10 days. They made an advance booking for their hotels in Paris, to avoid any last-minute trouble. However, on the day of the departure, they came to know that their flight had been cancelled due to bad weather. The next available flight is scheduled after a two-day delay. This news got Pravin worried, as the money spent on hotel booking in Paris is non-refundable, which meant he would have to spend more for additional bookings. In contrast, Prashant was calm and composed, as he had already made some arrangements to avoid such troubles. What arrangements did Prashant make? Let's find out in this chapter.

Insurance, in general terms, means protection. Any asset including house, car or even life has a risk associated with it. Insurance helps you to safeguard from the potential risks that may arise in the future. Insurance can be broadly classified into two categories:

1-General Insurance

2-Life Insurance

Let's see in detail about both the types

GENERAL INSURANCE

General insurance provides coverage for non-life assets in the event of loss due to fire, theft, burglary or any other unfortunate incident. The contract document containing the terms and conditions is called policy, and the defined amount of coverage is called sum insured. Some common types of general insurance products are as follows:

1) **Vehicle/Motor insurance** – All of us who own a car/two-wheeler must have taken vehicle insurance to avoid the penalties imposed by traffic police. Although we take it because it is compulsory, it becomes imperative to know the benefits of this insurance. There are various parties involved in vehicle insurance, which are as follows:

i- First party – The vehicle owner who pays the insurance premium (policyholder) is called the first party.

ii- Second party –The insurance company to whom the premium has been paid by vehicle owner is called second party.

iii- Third party –Any person other than the above two is called a third party.

While driving a vehicle, if you cause an accident that results in damage to another person's (third party's) life or property, the insurance company will pay for the damages on your behalf. This is called third-party insurance. These damages may include loss of life, injury, disability, property or vehicle damage etc. However, the damages incurred to your own vehicle will not be covered by this insurance. In India, it is mandatory to buy third-party insurance to drive a vehicle.

In addition to the third-party benefits, if you cover your own vehicle under insurance against damages, it is called first-party insurance. It is also known as comprehensive or package insurance. Any loss to your vehicle due to an accident, fire, theft or natural calamities (earthquake, flood, landslide etc.) is covered under comprehensive insurance. The premium amount for such insurance is higher than third-party insurance, but you can get various benefits with this added premium.

2) **Property Insurance –** Purchasing a property is a significant investment, and in the event of damage, it can result in a substantial financial loss. However, you can mitigate this risk by insuring the property. This type of insurance is called property insurance or home insurance.

For those who have obtained a loan to purchase the property, banks often make it mandatory to insure the property. You have the option of buying insurance from the bank itself or from any other insurance company of your choice. In the event of damage to the property, the insurance claim will directly go to your loan account. However, even if you haven't taken a loan to purchase the property, it is still advisable to obtain property insurance to protect against any financial loss.

Property insurance covers losses arising from fire, explosion, earthquake, storm, lightening, riot etc. During the claim, you will be reimbursed for cost of the building structure. Additionally, you can also insure the contents of your home, such as a TV, refrigerator and other valuable items like jewellery, silverware, and paintings by paying an additional premium in the property insurance.

3) **Health Insurance –** All investment planning takes a back seat if there is a medical emergency at home. To avoid such situations, it is crucial to have adequate health insurance coverage for yourself and your family members. Health insurance covers hospitalization expenses such as room rent, nursing charges, ICU charges, doctor fees, medicine charges and any other treatment-related costs.

Insurance companies make tie-ups with hospitals for the speedy disposal of claims. If treatment is received at such tie-up hospitals, the insurance company directly pays the bills for the treatment to the hospitals. This type of health insurance is called cashless insurance. However, if you receive treatment at a hospital that is not a part of tie-up network, you need to submit the claim form along with bills and the insurance company will reimburse the amount.

Many insurance policies have a clause regarding coverage for pre-existing diseases after a certain waiting period. For instance, if a person has asthma and wants to take health insurance, the claim for asthma treatment may not be included until a certain waiting period, such as 3- 4 years, as per policy conditions. However, if the person pays the premium regularly during those years, their asthma treatment will also be covered in the insurance after the completion of waiting period. In case the policyholder misses an insurance payment, the existing waiting period is not counted. Therefore, it is important to pay the premium regularly to keep the policy in force so that pre-existing diseases will also get covered in the future.

In addition to these benefits, you can claim a tax deduction for the premium amount under Section 80D, which is an added advantage of buying a health insurance.

4) **Travel Insurance –** This insurance provides coverage for various adversities that may occur during your travel. These adversities may include medical emergencies, loss of luggage/passport, flight cancellation and more. In case of medical emergencies, insurance companies will pay for the expenses. If you experience loss or damage to your luggage and its contents, the insurance company will reimburse the cost. In case the flight gets delayed beyond a certain period or gets cancelled, the insurance company will cover the additional expenses during that time. These expenses may include hotel booking charges (if you had to stay at a hotel during delay/cancellation or had booked a hotel at your destination) and the difference in ticket costs (if you had to book another flight). You can also claim the insurance amount if you had to cancel the trip due a medical or other emergency. This facility is available for both domestic and international flight travel.

Now you must have understood the example of Prashant and Pravin mentioned at the beginning of this chapter. In this case, Prashant can claim for the hotel booking charges from his insurance company, along with any other expenses he had to incur due to the flight cancellation.

Travel insurance can also be obtained for train travel. This facility is provided by IRCTC which covers hospitalization expenses, accidental damage, loss of life and more. The scheme is applicable only to Indian citizens who have booked their e-ticket through the online portal of IRCTC (NGeT website), and not to physical ticket booking at the counter. The premium for this service is below 1 rupee per person, which makes this insurance very affordable.

LIFE INSURANCE

Life insurance is a contract between an individual and insurance company, in which the company promises to pay a specified amount of money in the event of loss or damage to the insured person's life. The specified amount of insurance claim is called sum assured amount. Following are the types of life insurance:

1) Term Insurance – Term insurance is a pure protection plan in which the insurance claim is provided upon the death of the policyholder. It offers financial security to the family in the event of the unfortunate demise of the earning member. Ideally, the term insurance coverage should be around 10-15 times of the net annual income. For example, if a person earns Rs. 10 lakhs per year, the term insurance amount should be around Rs.1- 1.50 crores so that it can help to fulfil the monthly expenses and future needs of family. The term insurance can also be claimed in following situations:

Critical illness – There are certain illnesses that are life-threatening but can be cured if medical treatment is done. Such treatments require a lot of money. Term insurance claim can be raised to cover these treatment expenses. Every insurance company provides a list of critical illnesses that are covered under term insurance, which may include conditions like cancer, heart disease, kidney failure, lung disease etc.

Terminal illness – These are illnesses where the life expectancy of the policyholder is less than 12 months, as determined by medical reports. Examples of such illnesses include the advanced-stage cancer, advanced heart problems, neurological diseases etc. Insurance claim can be paid in the event of such terminal illnesses.

Disability – In addition to illnesses, there are certain total and permanent disabilities that prevent the policyholder from performing their work and earning income. These disabilities may include loss of arms/ legs, loss of eyesight or any neurological/mental condition that hinders normal functioning. In such cases, the insurance claim can be paid to provide for the future expenses of the family.

Suicide- Death by suicide is covered under term insurance after 1 year from the date of purchasing the policy

The basic insurance plan does not include all the features as mentioned earlier. To get insurance with the required features, a rider is provided by the insurance companies. In insurance, a rider refers to additional benefits that can be obtained by paying extra premiums. For example, some insurance companies cover only natural death in their basic plan whereas accidental death is not covered. In such cases, an accidental death benefit rider can be added by paying an additional premium. There are various such riders offered by insurance companies. Policy buyers should take into consideration such riders as per their requirements before buying the policy.

In a regular term insurance plan, premiums are to be paid throughout the term of the insurance. If the policyholder survives the insurance period, the premiums are not refunded. However, there is another variant of the term insurance, where if the policyholder survives the insurance period, the total premium paid is returned at the end of the term. This type of term insurance is called "return of premium" insurance, but the premium amount is higher than regular term insurance. There is also the option of "limited premium" insurance where premiums are paid for a shorter period than the actual insurance term. For example, a policy buyer can insure themselves for a period of 30 years but choose to pay premiums for the first 10 years only, while still receiving insurance coverage for the full 30 years. The premium for this variant is higher than that of a regular term insurance. Policy buyers can select the variant as per their choice.

2) **Loan Term Insurance –** This is another type of term insurance where banks provide insurance to cover the loan amount. When a person takes a home loan from a bank, the bank may ask the borrower to buy insurance to cover his loan. In the event of an unfortunate death of the borrower, the insurance company pays the entire outstanding loan amount to the bank, relieving the nominees from the burden of repaying the loan. The one-time premium for this insurance is added to the loan amount, and the borrower repays the loan as a part of the EMI. For example, if a person has taken a home loan of Rs. 50 lakhs and the premium for loan insurance is Rs. 1 lakh, the bank provides a total loan amount of Rs. 51 lakhs, and the borrower has to pay EMIs for the total amount of Rs. 51 lakhs.

There is a common misconception among many people that loan insurance is mandatory, which is false. Borrowers can refuse to buy the loan insurance. This type of insurance is recommended for people who do not have sufficient term insurance coverage. Those who already have term insurance can choose to enhance their coverage by adding the loan amount. For instance, if a person is already has a term insurance of Rs. 1 crore and is availing the loan of Rs. 50 lakhs, they can increase their term insurance cover to Rs. 1.50 crores by paying an additional premium. This way, their loan is secured along with the future financial needs of their family.

3) **Endowment Insurance Plans** – These are the type of insurance plans, where the life insurance is given along with an investment option. The sum assured is usually ten times of premium amount. For example, if the annual premium for endowment policy is Rs. 50000, the sum assured will be Rs. 5 lakhs, which is paid to the nominee in event of death of the policyholder. If the policyholder survives the insurance period, the premium amount is returned along with a bonus. The bonus usually falls in the range of 5-7% of total premium paid during the term of the insurance. The bonus percentage is guaranteed in this plan and is also mentioned in the policy document. These policies are commonly known as money-back plans, guaranteed plans or traditional plans.

4) **Unit Linked Insurance Policy (ULIP) –** Another variant similar to an endowment plan is ULIP. The sum assured is usually ten times of premium amount which is paid on the death or other events as discussed in term insurance. The premium paid by the policyholder is invested in bonds and equity market, so it functions like a mutual fund. Since the premium amount is invested in debt and equity funds, the return on investment generally falls within the range of 8-10%. The final amount received at the end of policy term is tax-free under section 10 (10D) of Income Tax Act, which is applicable for both ULIPs and endowment plans.

Though ULIPs may initially seem attractive, it is advised not to mix insurance with investment for the following reasons:

i- Inadequate insurance cover - In ULIPs or endowment plans, the sum assured is typically 10-15 times of premium amount, which is very less than that of term insurance. This defeats the whole purpose of insurance, as the sum assured is not sufficient to meet the future needs of a family. Moreover, the premium of term insurance is much lower compared to these investment policies.

ii- Return on investment – Endowment plans offer returns in the range of 5-7%, which can also be achieved through fixed deposits

(FDs) in banks. ULIPs provide returns in the range of 8-10 %, which can be attained through mutual funds or stock market.

iii- Lock in period – ULIPs have a minimum lock-in period of 5 years, making it difficult to withdraw the funds in case of emergencies. Similarly, in endowment plans, if the policyholder tries to surrender the policy before maturity, the original investment amount is also not refunded.

iv- **Expense ratio** – As we have discussed in mutual funds, the expense ratio is usually around 1% for direct mutual fund plans. Whereas, in these policies, there are various charges such as mortality charge, fund management charge, premium allocation charge, premium discontinuance charge etc. These charges affect the return on investment hence mutual fund can be preferred over these insurance policies.

It is important to note that "insurance is a subject matter of solicitation", which means that insurance must be requested by an individual and cannot be sold to anyone without their permission. However, nowadays, a lot of mis-selling is happening with these insurance policies by insurance brokers, agents and banks. Incorrect product descriptions are provided to customers to lure them into buying these policies, and sometimes, the policies are even sold forcibly. Bank employees sell the policies to the loan-seeking customers, or they threaten customers that their loans will not be sanctioned. Such practices are now thriving in all banks. In some cases, customers who have long standing relationships with the banks are asked to buy these policies in order to help employees achieve their target. Additionally, close relatives who works an insurance agent may also urge you to buy the policy. While it is advised to avoid such situations but if at all any such case arise, and you are to buy the policy, you can chose the best possible policy by considering the following factors:

i- **Have adequate term insurance –** First, ensure that you have adequate term insurance to secure the future needs of the family then only you should consider about investing in ULIPs. If all your finances are in order and your investment portfolio is properly maintained, you can invest the surplus amount in ULIPs.

ii- Tax benefit – The premium amount invested in ULIPs or endowment policies can be deducted from tax under Section 80C. Additionally, the final amount received at the end of the insurance term is also exempted from tax under Section 10(10D). Therefore, if needed, it can be used as a tax-saving instrument.

iii- Allocate the funds –In ULIPs, the premium amount is invested in both equity and debt. Policyholders can decide the percentage of allocation based on their risk appetite. Insurance companies provide the option to switch funds. Therefore, at any point of time, you can switch your funds from debt to equity or vice versa. You can check the performance of the investment and switch your funds accordingly.

iv-Avoid endowment policy – If you have to choose between endowment plans and ULIPs, you should go for ULIPs. Although, endowment plans offer guaranteed returns, the returns are typically very low, making it a poor investment product. On the other hand, ULIPs provide higher returns as they function in a similar manner to mutual funds.

v- Waiver of premium – Some ULIP plans comes with the benefit of "waiver of premium". For instance, there are various child plans in which a parent can make the investment for the future needs of a child. Usually in insurance policies, the insurance cover is valid as long as the policyholder is alive and paying the premium. However, in these plans, in the event of the death of the policyholder, the sum assured amount is given to the nominee and the policy does not end. The remaining premiums are then paid by the insurance company until the end of the term, and the child receives the total amount upon maturity. Since the maturity amount is tax-free, these policies can be considered as an alternative to the Sukanya Samriddhi Account, as these policies can be availed for both boys and girls.

With this, we will now move on to the final product of life insurance.

5) **Pension Plan –** As the name suggests, this plan is designed to provide a pension to the policyholder. Usually, these plans do not have insurance coverage; instead, their goal is to provide an annuity (pension). As we discussed in NPS, the investment amount, along with the interest, is used to provide a pension to subscriber. Similarly, you can invest in pension plan to receive the pension. On the basis of the annuity period, the pension plan is divided into two categories:

i- Deferred Annuity – In this type of plan, you invest the money at regular intervals for a certain years, and the pension starts after the investment period is over. For example, if you wish to have a pension after 10 years, you would invest a certain amount monthly or yearly for 10 years, and the pension payment would begin from the 11th year onward. The pension amount will depend on the amount invested and the interest received on the invested amount. This amount is called "purchase price".

Instead of making regular investment, you can also choose to invest lump-sum amount in a deferred annuity plan. For example, if you invest Rs. 20 lakhs lump-sum amount in a pension plan, and you wish to receive the pension after 5 years, the invested amount of Rs. 20 lakhs will receive interest for 5 years. Depending on its value at the end of 5 years, you will start receiving the pension from 6th year onwards.

ii- Immediate Annuity – In this category, you invest a lump-sum amount to purchase the annuity plan, the pension will start immediately from the next month.

On the basis of the pension beneficiary, the pension plan can be divided into following four categories:

i- Annuity for life with ROP – In this type, the primary policyholder will receive a pension for their lifetime. Upon the death of the policyholder, the pension will stop and the entire purchase price amount will be returned to nominee. Here, the purchase price is returned to the nominee, hence it is called ROP (return of purchase price).

ii- Joint life annuity with ROP – In this category, the primary policyholder will receive a pension for lifetime. In the event of the death of the policyholder, the pension will be payable to the spouse for their lifetime. Upon the death of the spouse, the pension will stop, and the entire purchase price will be returned to the nominee.

iii- Annuity for life without ROP – In this category, the primary policyholder will receive a pension for their lifetime. Upon the death of the policyholder, the pension will stop, and no further amount will be payable.

iv- Joint life annuity without ROP – In this category, the primary policyholder will receive a pension for their lifetime. In the event of the death of the policyholder, the pension will be payable to the spouse for their lifetime. On the death of the spouse, the pension will stop, and no further amount will be payable.

In the NPS (National Pension System), the final corpus amount is used to purchase a pension plan of an insurance company. Subscribers are given an option to choose a pension plan from various insurance companies. The chosen insurance company will then provide the pension to the subscriber. The pension amount can be checked using the pension calculators available on the websites of insurance companies.

We have covered all the important insurance products. To ensure you choose the best available product in market and maximize your benefits, keep the following things in mind when selecting an insurance policy:

i-Try to buy the policy online- The premiums are typically lower when you purchase the policy online. This is because when you buy the policy from agents or banks, you also pay for their commission, which increases the premium. Buying the policy directly from the insurance company's official website cut the cost of middlemen and you get the policy at a lower premium.

ii- Always check for exclusions in policy – Not every insurance company offers all the benefits in their basic plan. Sometimes, you need to pay an additional premium for extra benefits. Therefore, it becomes important to check for such exclusions which are not covered in their basic plan. Moreover, each insurance company may offer different benefit compared to others. For example, in property insurance, some companies may cover the cost of house (building), whereas other companies might cover the cost of the home appliances along with the cost of the house. Hence, comparing the benefits of different companies can save you a lot of premiums.

iii- Adequate cover – Insurance is intended to protect you from the future losses, so it is essential to obtain adequate insurance which sufficiently covers the cost of your assets. While some people tend to buy a policy with the least premium, but such policies may not provide full coverage for the entire cost of the asset. This can lead to financial losses in the event of any mishap or accident.

iv- Choosing the best company- There are various insurance companies in market, so choosing the best company becomes a difficult task. One parameter which can help while buying insurance is the "claim settlement ratio". This ratio indicates the percentage of claims settled by the company out of total claims received. Insurance companies typically provide their claim settlement ratios on their website. By choosing the company with a higher claim settlement ratio, you can ensure a smoother claim process.

v- Furnish the correct details – Insurance companies might deny the claim if you have provided inaccurate or incomplete details while buying the policy. These details may include your age, medical history, pre-existing diseases, lifestyle habits or any other details. It is important to furnish correct and complete details to avoid any claim rejection in the future. You can cross-verify those details when you receive the insurance policy. If any mismatch or discrepancy found in policy documents, you can ask the insurance company to rectify the data and provide you with updated policy documents.

vi- Timely claim – Certain insurance companies or specific insurance products have the condition regarding submitting the claim within a certain stipulated period. If you fail to submit your claim within the stipulated period, the claim might get rejected. Therefore it is advised to file the claim promptly to avoid any rejection.

vii- Cancelling the policy – Customers are given a period of around 15-30 days to review the terms and conditions of the policy, and cancel the policy if not acceptable. This period is called the "free look period". If you cancel the policy during the free look period, the premium is refunded by insurance companies after deducting some nominal charges. However, once this period is over, the policyholder cannot avail this facility. If you feel that the product was mis-sold or accurate product information was not provided, you can cancel the insurance during this period to avoid any losses.

With this, we conclude the chapter on insurance. We will now proceed to the next chapter.

CHAPTER 7

NPA & CREDIT REPORTS (CIBIL)

Neerav had taken a car loan of Rs. 5 lakhs from the bank 3 years ago, and the remaining outstanding loan amount is currently Rs. 3.50 lakhs. However, due to certain reasons, Neerav stopped paying the EMIs and the loan has turned into an NPA. The bank sent several notices to Neerav, but he did not pay. What steps will be taken by bank in this case, and how will it affect Neerav, let's find out in this chapter.

When the bank gives a loan to a customer, it earns interest on that loan, thus a loan becomes an asset for the bank. As long as the customer pays the EMI, the loan is treated as a standard or performing asset. However, if the customer fails to pay the EMIs, it becomes a Non-Performing Asset (NPA) for the bank. Typically, a loan account becomes NPA when the borrower fails to pay three consecutive EMIs. In such cases, banks initiate the recovery process in following ways:

i- After the first EMI is due, bank sends a reminder through a call/SMS to the borrower for regularizing the loan account.

ii- If the account is not regularized even after sending the reminder, a notice is sent to the borrower.

iii- During or before the account turns NPA, bank staff or recovery agents employed by the bank visit the borrower to persuade them to regularize the loan account.

iv- If all such recovery efforts are failed and borrower is not repaying the loan, the bank initiates legal action against the borrower. If the EMI is being paid through ECS or cheque, the bank may file a case of ECS/cheque bounce, and a court case can be filed against the borrower. Additionally, if the loan has collateral security (house, car etc.), the bank also starts the process of seizing the collateral.

v- The seized asset is then sold through a public auction. The money received from the auction is used to close the loan account. If the money received from auction exceeds the outstanding loan amount, the remaining amount is returned to the borrower. However, if the amount received is less, the borrower is asked to repay the remaining amount to close the account.

vi- If the borrower does not pay the remaining amount, the bank writes off the loan amount.

Write-off is a process in which the bank closes the original loan account and opens a separate account for the un-received amount. For example, in Neerav's case, if all other recovery efforts fail, the bank will auction the car. Assuming that the bank has auctioned the car and received Rs. 3 lakhs after the sale, the bank will credit that amount to the loan account. However, since the current outstanding of loan is Rs. 3.50 lakhs, the bank will ask Neerav to pay the remaining amount of Rs. 50,000 to close the loan account. If he does not pay the remaining amount, the bank will open a new loan account of Rs. 50,000 and close his original car loan account. In this case, the amount of Rs. 50,000 is written-off by the bank. Although bank may not stress much on recovering the written-off amount, Neerav is still liable to pay Rs. 50,000 to the bank (Contrary to the belief that write-off means the loan is waived, it actually means that the bank has reduced its recovery measures because chances of loan recovery is now less).

In addition to the issues mentioned above, various charges are also imposed on the borrower if the EMIs are not paid on time.

i-Penal interest – When the EMIs are not paid on time, a penalty is imposed which is called penal interest. The amount of penal interest can be 2-4% per month of the overdue amount. For example, if your home loan EMI is Rs. 50000 and you missed the EMI for one month, then an additional penal interest of 2% of the overdue amount (2% of Rs. 50,000 which is Rs. 1000) is charged on your EMI. This penal interest is charged every month till the account becomes regular.

ii- ECS failure charges – If the ECS gets bounced due to certain reasons, ECS failure charges are also applied. For example; let's assume that you have taken a loan from ABC bank and your salary account is in XYZ bank. Your EMI is automatically deducted from your salary account on 10th day of each month. If the EMI could not be deducted on 10th day, XYZ bank (salary account bank) will deduct ECS failure charges for that failed transaction. These charges can be from Rs. 250 to Rs. 500 (plus GST). Hence it is advised to keep sufficient balance in your account on the due date of EMI.

iii- Legal and other fees – If the loan account becomes NPA, the bank hires an advocate to initiate legal action against the borrower. Additionally, banks may also hire recovery agents for the recovery of loans. In the case of auctions, banks are required to publish advertisements in newspapers regarding auctions. The fees for advocates, recovery agents, and expenses for newspaper ads can be recovered from the borrowers.

To avoid such situations, it is crucial to keep the loan regular. A much-needed thought should be given before availing any loan. Although there might be some factors such as loss of job or medical emergencies which might affect loan repayment but keeping the EMI within the prescribed limit of salary can help avoid these hassles. If it becomes difficult to pay the EMIs, it is advised to visit the bank and inform them about such situation. Depending upon the repayment history, the bank might provide a solution in such situations. For example, during the COVID crisis, borrowers were given the option of a moratorium, allowing them to extend their EMI date by a few months.

Another major drawback of NPA is that it negatively affects your credit score. A credit score is calculated by considering factors such as the number of loans, amount of loans, repayment history and various other factors. These scores are determined by various companies, including CIBIL, CRIF, Equifax, Experian etc. These companies are known as Credit Information Companies (CIC). The most well-known among these companies is CIBIL, which stands for Credit Information Bureau (India) Ltd. Although people commonly refer to these reports as CIBIL reports, but the actual name for such reports is Credit Information Report (CIR) or simply credit report.

The score of each credit report is given between 300 to 900 marks, where 300 is the lowest and 900 is the highest score. Customers with low scores are considered high-risk customers, while those with high scores are considered low-risk customers. Banks examine these reports when giving loans to customers. If a customer has good repayment history and a high credit score, it becomes easier for them to get their loan sanctioned. We will now try to understand the credit reports in detail. The following terms are used in the credit report:

i - **Standard (STD)** – It indicates that the EMIs are paid regularly, and the loan is considered a standard asset.

ii- **Special Mention Account (SMA)** – It means that more than one but less than three EMIs are pending, and the account is moving towards becoming NPA.

iii- **Sub-standard (SUB)** – It means three or more EMIs are pending, and the loan account has turned into an NPA.

iv- **Doubtful (DBT)** – It means that the loan account has been an NPA for more than 12 months.

v- **Loss (LSS)** - It means the loan account has been written off.

vi- **Days Past Due (DPD)** - It denotes the number of days by which the EMI is missed. For example, if a person has missed EMIs for two months, then the DPD will be shown as 60 days. In standard accounts, DPD will be shown as zero whereas in SMA, SUB, DBT and LSS, it will be shown as the number of days the EMI is not paid. We will explore this in detail in the following images. A sample of credit report is as follows:

As shown in image 1, the credit report is divided into 5 parts.

1-Score- The score is displayed on the top of the report, along with it the corresponding risk category. A score above 700 is considered low risk, while a score below 500 is considered high risk for banks.

2- Personal Information- This section includes personal details such as contact number, address and identification details (such as PAN Card, Aadhar Card numbers). These details are used to fetch the credit report.

3- Summary-A brief summary of all the loans taken is mentioned here. It displays the number of accounts that have been closed and those that are currently running. The total sanctioned amount and current outstanding amount is also mentioned. In image 1, for example, the customer has taken a total of three loans amounting to Rs. 15 lakhs. Two loans have been closed and are shown as zero balance loans, while one loan is still active with an outstanding amount of Rs. 8 lakhs.

CONSUMER CIR

CONSUMER INFORMATION:

NAME: ALBERT PINTO
DATE OF BIRTH: 01/01/1975 GENDER: MALE

SCORE	750	LOW RISK

IDENTIFICATION(S)

IDENTIFICATION TYPE	IDENTIFICATION NUMBER
INCOME TAX ID NUMBER (PAN)	ABCDE2022G
UNIVERSAL ID NUMBER (UID)	123456789012

MOBILE NUMBER	9876543210
E-MAIL ID	ALBERTPINTO@CREDIT.COM
ADDRESS	HOUSE NO-1, SECOND ROAD, 3RD SQUARE, DELHI

SUMMARY

ACCOUNT	ADVANCES	BALANCE
Total -3 Ovedue- 0 Zero Balance- 2	15,00,000	8,00,000

DETAILED REPORT OF EACH LOAN ACCOUNT
(AS SHOWN IN NEXT IMAGES)

Enquiries done in past

MEMBER	ENQUIRY DATE	ENQUIRY PURPOSE	ENQUIRY AMOUNT
ABC BANK	01/01/2020	CAR LOAN	5,00,000
XYZ BANK	01/06/2020	CREDIT CARD	70,000
BANK OF ABC	01/06/2021	HOME LOAN	65,00,000
EFG BANK LTD.	10/06/2021	HOME LOAN	65,00,000

Image 1

4- Account information- This section provides detailed information about each account, including the type of loan, loan amount, sanction date and repayment history. More details will be shown in next images.

5- Enquiry information- This part displays the detail of credit report enquiries made in the past. Whenever a person applies for a loan, banks fetch their credit report. The date of enquiry and types of loans for which customer has approached the bank are mentioned here.

Now we will see how account information is given in next image.

Account Type: CONSUMER LOAN | **Info as of : 01/08/2022**

Ownership: INDIVIDUAL | **Disbursed Date: 01/01/2020** | **Disbd Amt: 45000**

Instl Amt/ Freq: 1800/Monthly | **Last Paid Date: 01/07/2022** | **Overdue Amt: 0**

Status: CLOSED | **Tenure: 30 months** | **Current Balance: 0**

Payment History/ Asset Classification

	JANUARY	FEBRUARY	MARCH	APRIL	MAY	JUNE	JULY	AUGUST	SEPTEMEBER	OCTOBER	NOVEMBER	DECEMBER
2022	000/STD	000/STD	000/STD	000/STD	000/STD	000/STD	000/STD					
2021	000/STD	000/STD	000/STD	000/STD	000/STD	000/STD	000/STD	000/STD	000/STD	000/STD	000/STD	000/STD
2020		000/STD	000/STD	000/STD	000/STD	000/STD	000/STD	000/STD	000/STD	000/STD	000/STD	000/STD

Image 2

Taking a close look at image 2, you can see that the customer has availed a consumer loan of Rs. 45000 (disbursed amount) on 01/01/2020 with an EMI of Rs. 1800. The loan status is now closed and the date of closure is 01/07/2022. If you take a look at the repayment history, the days past due (DPD) in each month is zero which means the account was regular (standard). Such repayment history is considered good, and it increases the credit score. Now let's take a look at the next image.

Account Type: PERSONAL LOAN | **Info as of : 31/12/2015**

Ownership: INDIVIDUAL | **Disbursed Date: 01/01/2012** | **Disbd Amt: 500000**

Instl Amt/Freq: 11200/Monthly | **Last Paid Date: 01/01/2014** | **Overdue Amt: 250000**

Status: Written-off | **Tenure: 60 months** | **Writeoff Amt: 250000**

Payment History/ Asset Classification

	JANUARY	FEBRUARY	MARCH	APRIL	MAY	JUNE	JULY	AUGUST	SEPTEMEBER	OCTOBER	NOVEMBER	DECEMBER
2015	361/SUB	391/DBT	421/DBT	451/DBT	481/LOS	511/LOS						
2014	000/STD	031/SMA	061/SMA	091/SUB	121/SUB	151/SUB	181/SUB	211/SUB	241/SUB	271/SUB	301/SUB	331/SUB
2013	000/STD	000/STD	000/STD	000/STD	000/STD	000/STD	000/STD	000/STD	000/STD	000/STD	000/STD	000/STD
2012		000/STD	000/STD	000/STD	000/STD	000/STD	000/STD	000/STD	000/STD	000/STD	000/STD	000/STD

Image 3

In this image, you will find that the customer has availed a personal loan of Rs. 5 lakhs on 01/01/2012 having an EMI of Rs. 11200. As you can see, the repayment was regular for first two years till 01/01/2014, hence the DPD until that period is zero. However, the customer has not paid any EMIs since then, hence his DPD keeps increasing with each month. The account becomes SMA followed by substandard, then doubtful and finally the bank has decided to write off the account. As a result, the account status is now shown as WRITTEN-OFF. The write-off amount of Rs. 2,50,000 is also mentioned in the report. The reports which contain other than standard (STD) in repayment history tend to reduce the credit score. These customers are considered high-risk for banks and it becomes difficult for them to get loans in future.

In addition to these reports, there are customers who have never availed any loan in the past. The credit reports of these customers show a score of -1 (minus 1). While a -1 score is considered good, some banks may hesitate to approve loans for such customers as they are unable to examine their track record. To avoid this situation, one can consider applying for a loan of a lower value and ensure timely repayment to create a healthy credit score. This will provide banks with a track record to evaluate and increase likelihood of loan approvals in future.

When approving a loan, banks usually review credit reports from 2 different companies. Any two companies among CIBIL, CRIF, Equifax and Experian are selected for the credit report. This is done as additional safety check for banks, as the data in one report might not be reflected in another report. The lower score between the two reports is taken into consideration when sanctioning the loan. Nowadays, the interest rate of the loan is determined based on the credit score. Customers with higher credit score can get the loan at lower interest rates. Therefore, a good credit score can help you save the EMIs.

Occasionally, it may happen that the credit reports contain information which is not relevant to you. For example, your credit report might contain a loan which was not availed by you or there might be a loan which was closed long time ago but not updated in the report. Such errors can affect your credit score negatively. For rectification of such errors, a dispute resolution link is given on the official website of the credit information companies. Such disputes are then resolved by the companies and the credit report is updated with the relevant information.

While everyone aims to maintain a good credit score, there are some mistakes which can negatively impact the credit score. The following are the most common reasons for a reduction in credit score:

1-Credit Card- One of the common reasons for a low credit score is improper usage of credit card. There are various factors associated with the use of credit card.

a- Bill payment on due date- Not paying the bills on due date reduces the credit score of a card holder.

b- Partial payment- Sometimes, people only pay the minimum due amount rather than full bill amount. This practice reduces the credit score.

c- High credit usage- Even if the full bill is paid on time, using more than 30% of the credit limit affects your credit score. For example, if the credit card limit is Rs. 1 lakhs, the credit usage in a billing cycle should not exceed Rs. 30000.

d- Other issues- Occasionally, people obtain a credit card but do not use it. However, the annual maintenance charges of card are to be paid even if the card is not used. If these charges are not paid, credit card companies might charge an additional interest on that unpaid amount and the charges keeps increasing. On non-payment, companies might write off these charges but it eventually affects your credit score. Therefore, it is advised to pay these charges even if the card is not used or you can call the card helpline number and block the card so that these charges are not levied on you.

Sometimes, there are disputes regarding the bill amount. Such disputes should be quickly resolved otherwise the bill amount gets increased over the period of time. You can file a complaint to regulating authorities for quick disposal of such disputes so that it might not affect your credit score.

2- Credit Score Enquiry- If a person applies for a loan at multiple banks, each bank will generate a credit report. Having multiple enquiries from different banks indicates that the consumer is credit-hungry; this in turn reduces the credit score.

There are two types of inquiries related to the credit score. When you check your own credit score, it is called as soft enquiry and it does not affect the credit score. However, if the banks/F.I. checks your credit score, it is called hard inquiry which may affect your credit score negatively. These inquiries are displayed in the inquiry section of the credit report (as shown in image 1). Therefore, it is advisable not to apply for a loan at multiple banks simultaneously.

3- Guarantor- People often become guarantors for others without realizing the true meaning of it. As per RBI guidelines, if a borrower fails to repay a loan, it becomes the guarantor's responsibility to repay that loan. Banks can use all the applicable recovery methods in such cases against the guarantor. This means that guarantor is equally liable for the loan. So, if the original borrower defaults the loan, it also affects the credit score of guarantor. For these reasons, it is advised to avoid taking the guarantee of someone's loan unless you are ready to pay their loan if any problems arise. A guarantor should also keep the track of whether the original borrower is paying the EMIs on time.

5- Loan waiver schemes- Sometimes, the government announces loan waiver schemes for specific borrowers. For example, a few years back, agriculture loans of farmers in the state of Maharashtra were waived due to drought. The scheme was applicable only to small and marginal farmers who did not have any income other than farming. However, many people did not pay their agriculture loans in the hope that they would be waived. The decision adversely affected their credit scores, and ultimately, their loans also were not waived.

Another issue with such loan waiver schemes is the significant amount of time it takes to carry out the waiver process. It typically takes around 1 year or more from the announcement of the waiver scheme to actually waive the loans. During this period, the loan remains unpaid, and it affects the credit score. Although, loan waiver schemes are granted for small value loans but the impact it creates on the future loans can be huge. To understand it more clearly, let's take a look at the home loan interest rates of a leading bank in our country as of October 2022.

CREDIT SCORE	INTEREST RATE
>= 800	8.55%
750-799	8.65%
700-749	8.75%
650-699	8.85%
550-649	9.05%
NTC/NO CIBIL SCORE/ -1	8.75%

Image 4

As you can see in the image, people with a credit score of 800 and above will be charged an interest rate of 8.55%. On the other hand, for those with a score ranging from 550-649, the interest rate will be 9.05%, which is 0.50% higher than the minimum rate. When you calculate the impact of this 0.50% on your EMI, you will find a difference of lakhs of rupees which could have otherwise been saved. Hence, it is advised to keep the loans regular and enjoy the benefits of reduced interest rates.

6- **Settlement of loans** – If a loan account remains NPA for a longer period, banks offer borrowers a settlement option. In these settlements, bank waives a certain portion of the loan so that the remaining amount of loan can be recovered. For example, let's assume that a person has taken a personal loan of Rs. 4 lakhs, with a current outstanding amount of Rs. 3 lakhs, and is unable to pay further. Since there is no collateral security with the bank hence the chances of recovery are slim. In such cases, bank may offer a settlement scheme to borrower where the bank will waive some amount, let's say Rs. 1 lakh, and ask the borrower to pay the remaining amount of Rs. 2 lakhs to close the loan. Although this may seem like a favourable option to the borrower, as they do not have to pay the entire outstanding amount, but doing so affects the credit score of borrower. The waived amount is written-off by bank and reflected in the credit report as "SETTLED". For this reason, it is advised to avoid the settlements and instead pay the entire dues for a good credit score.

7- Proper payment channel of EMI- Many banks and financial institutions employ outside agencies for recovery of loans. These recovery agents are usually part time employees hired on a contract basis. They visit the borrower for recovery of loans, and sometimes they collect the EMI amount in cash. However, in some cases, it is observed that the agents do not deposit the EMI to the bank. As a result, even if you have paid the EMI, it may still show as pending in the bank records. So if any EMI is missed, it should be paid either from account/cheque or by cash in the authorized branches of banks and collect the proper receipt of the payment otherwise you may lose money and it will also affect the credit score.

If above mistakes are avoided, you can maintain a healthy credit score. A good credit score will help you to avail loans easily and probably with a lower interest rate. With this, now we will move on to our next chapter.

CHAPTER 8

FRAUDS & COMPLAINT RESOLUTION

Miss Pooja is a businesswoman residing in Mumbai. A few days ago, she withdrew some money from the nearby ATM machine. However, on the same day, some unauthorized transactions were made using her card. She reported the incident to the bank, and upon investigation, it was discovered that the ATM machine had a skimming device installed by fraudsters. The total amount debited from her account was Rs. 30,000. In this chapter, we will learn about how to prevent such frauds and the necessary steps to take when faced with such situations.

With the advent of technology, online transactions have become more convenient. Along with the internet banking, various UPI apps are also available in the market which facilitates the ease of transactions. However, the rise in online transactions has also led to an increase in online frauds. Various fraud techniques are used by scammers to deceive the customers. Some well-known methods are as follows:

1) Phishing- In this method, scammers send an e-mail to the customer with an attachment containing a link. Upon clicking the link, a virus gets downloaded into the system, which steals sensitive data, leading to financial fraud. This type of fraud technique is known as phishing, and if such links are sent through SMS, it is called SMS phishing (smishing). Sometimes, scammers may even pose as bank employees and call the individuals to obtain their bank details, this method is known as voice phishing (vishing). To protect yourself from such situations, it is advised not to click on any unauthorized links and to have a reliable antivirus installed on your phone or laptop that can detect and remove the virus. Along with this, it is always important to use only authorized websites of the banks, e-commerce platforms, and financial portals and to check the secure sign (http**s** with a padlock symbol) in the URL before entering any banking credentials.

2) Card Skimming- Scammers install a skimming device in the ATM. When you swipe your card in such a machine, your card data gets stolen, leading to the fraud. To avoid this, it is advised to check the card slot machine for any skimming device before making a transaction. You can do this by slightly wiggling the card slot and checking the slot for any tape or sticky glue residue. Another way to avoid card skimming is by card-less cash withdrawals. Nowadays, many banks are providing this facility where you can withdraw the money from ATM without using the ATM card. A reference number is generated which enables you to withdraw the money from ATM. You can contact your bank for activation of this facility to safeguard yourself from the frauds related to card skimming.

3) UPI fraud- In this type of fraud, scammers send a QR code to the users, asking them to scan the code to receive the payment. However, once the user scans the code, it asks them to put their UPI pin. After the pin is entered, the amount gets deducted from their account. It is important to note that in UPI transactions, the QR code is to be scanned only for making a payment and never for receiving any money.

4) Credit Card- Fraudsters call you posing as the employee of the credit card company, and requests your card details for various services such as activation of card, limit upgrade, cash-back offers, KYC update, and more. Once the card details are provided, they ask for One-Time Password (OTP) to authorize the process, and subsequently, the amount is deducted. It should always be remembered that no company will ever ask for your personal details or OTP. It is always safe to call on the authorized helpline number of the company to avail any information regarding the services offered by them.

5) Online Job offers- A message is sent on your phone regarding a fake job offer. An online interview is conducted as part of the selection process. After being selected, fraudsters ask you to send the money for various reasons such as completing the registration process/paperwork, training fees or even for providing a laptop. In such cases, it is essential to verify the genuineness of the company before applying for any online jobs and always remember that a genuine company never ask money in exchange for a job offer.

6) Data Entry Jobs- In this type of fraud, the same process as mentioned previously is used but the fraudsters do not ask for money during the selection stage. They assign the data entry work to you and give you a deadline of 8-10 days to complete the task. Along with that, a condition is imposed that the data submitted by you must be error-free. Once you submit the work, they contact you and claim that the data submitted by you contained a lot of errors, due to which their client had to face a financial loss. At this point, they ask you to compensate for the loss or face the legal action. A fake legal notice is also sent to your e-mail to scare you into paying the money. In such cases, you can rest assured that these are just hoaxes, and nobody can take any action against you. To be more on a safe side, you also can lodge a complaint against them with police department.

7) Juice Jacking- Often, we charge our mobile phones in public places such as cafes, airports, and railway stations. Fraudsters keep their charging cables in these places. If you charge the phone using these cables, the phone gets hacked by these fraudsters and sensitive information such as SMS, emails, passwords can be accessed by them. To prevent such situations, it is advised not to use public or unknown charging ports. If you must use them in emergency situations, always use your own data cable for charging.

8) Online Lottery- A message is sent on your phone that you have won the lottery. Once you contact the fraudsters, they ask you to transfer the money to pay for taxes/ charges/registration fees etc. for receiving the lottery money. Since, these are all fake lotteries; it is prudent to completely ignore all such messages.

9) Loan Apps- Scammers create fake loan apps and attract customers by promising loans at very low-interest rates. In this type of fraud, customers are either asked to pay processing fees upfront or sensitive data is stolen by scammers after downloading the app. The list of authorized loan apps is given on the website of Reserve Bank of India hence you should always check the authenticity of such apps before downloading.

10) Sim Swapping/Sim Cloning- This is one sophisticated method of fraud where the fraudster calls posing as an employee of a Telecom Company. They ask you to upgrade your SIM card for better connectivity (4G/5G) or for a better monthly plan. To activate the service, they then ask for information such as your Aadhar card number and ICCID (Integrated Circuit Card ID) number, which is printed on the SIM card. Once this information is provided, the scammers get full control of your SIM card, and they can access all the messages received on your SIM card, which leads to fraud. To avoid such incidents, it is advised to contact the authorized centre of the telecom company regarding any changes to the SIM card and not to disclose any information over the phone.

These were some common types of online fraud techniques used by scammers to steal money. We have also discussed the methods to avoid falling victim to them. However, if any unfortunate incident of fraud happens, the following steps should be taken which can help you retrieve the money:

1) When you receive an SMS or e-mail regarding an unauthorized transaction from your account, you need to immediately report it to your bank. The transaction SMS contains the helpline number for registering the complaint. As per the RBI guidelines, once the complaint is registered, it becomes the responsibility of the bank to prevent next such transactions. If any unauthorized transaction takes place after reporting, then that subsequent loss will be borne by the bank.

2) After reporting to the bank, you should report the incident to the cybercrime division by calling their helpline number, 1930.If the reporting is done within 1 hour from the time of the transaction, the chances of retrieving the money increase, as the cyber crime department can freeze the account of the scammers before they withdraw the amount. A separate portal has also been created for lodging such complaints which can be accessed at https://cybercrime.gov.in .

RBI has also issued guidelines to the banks regarding online fraud. Here are the key points:

i- In cases, where the unauthorized transaction has happened due to the fault of customer, the bank is not liable to compensate the customer. However, if the transaction has happened due to negligence or deficiency on the part of the bank, the bank has to pay entire amount to the customer within 10 days of receiving the complaint.

ii- In cases, where the transaction has happened but the deficiency lies neither with the bank nor with the customer, but lies elsewhere in the system, and the customer notifies the bank within 3 working days from the date of transaction, the bank is liable to pay the entire amount to the customer. Hence, it becomes important to report the transaction to the bank with utmost priority.

iii- In cases, where the complaint is either rejected by bank or remains unresolved for more than 30 days, and if you are certain that the negligence was not on your part, you can escalate the complaint to the Banking Ombudsman (BO). The BO is a specific regulated entity created by RBI to resolve the complaints related to the banking industry. The complaint can be registered under the grievance redressal section of the RBI website https://rbi.org.in .

iv- If the complaint registered at the bank remains unresolved for more than 90 days, the bank is liable to pay the full or partial amount to the customer, as per the guidelines prescribed by RBI.

To have an additional layer of protection against such frauds, you can opt for cyber security insurance. Several insurance companies have come up with this product, where the company will reimburse the loss amount in the event of any cyber fraud. Purchasing such insurance can help safeguard you from the losses incurred due to online frauds and you can have a relaxed mindset while conducting online transactions.

Apart from fraud, there are various other matters which can arise in the financial world. To resolve such issues, regulatory bodies are appointed by the government. A list of such regulatory bodies is given along with their respective portal address, which can help you to raise any complaints related to them:

1-Reserve Bank of India (RBI) - RBI is the regulatory body for all the banking-related services in India. It also regulates the government bond market in India. The issues related to banks, financial institutions (F.I), non-banking financial companies (NBFC), and government bonds can be raised on the portal of RBI. Along with this, Banking Ombudsman services can also be accessed through this portal: https://rbi.org.in .

2- Securities & Exchange Board of India (SEBI) -SEBI regulates the share market, corporate bond market and mutual funds in India. The complaints related to them can be raised on its website: https://sebi.gov.in .

3- Pension Fund Regulatory & Development Authority (PFRDA) - It is a regulatory body for NPS. Issues related to NPS can be raised from the grievance redressal section of the portal: https://pfrda.org.in .

4- Insurance Regulatory & Development Authority (IRDA) - It regulates the insurance sector of India. Rules and regulations related to insurance can be accessed from their portal: https://irdai.gov.in . They also have a separate insurance ombudsman portal which can be accessed through: https://policyholder.gov.in . Issues related to mis-selling, claim rejection, delay in claims, unsatisfactory settlement, and more can be raised through this portal.

5 – Deposit Insurance & Credit Guarantee Corporation (DICGC) -It is a specialized division of RBI that provides insurance coverage for bank deposits. If a bank gets insolvent and fails to pay the money to the depositors, DICGC pays the depositors their principal amount with interest, up to Rs. 5 lakhs. The grievance redressal section and the list of banks covered under the DICGC can be accessed from the portal: https://dicgc.org.in .

With this, we have finished our chapter. Hope this information will help you in resolving the issues related to financial world, and increase your awareness of your rights as a consumer. Now, let's proceed to the final chapter of our book.

CHAPTER 9
LEGACY

While working at a rural branch, I came across a strange situation one day. An elderly lady brought an FD receipt which was done by her deceased husband. The fixed deposit was more than 10 years old, and the lady informed me that she found the receipt while sorting through old documents. She wanted to know whether the FD was still active, or if it was closed by her husband.

While checking the FD details, I found that it was closed but the amount was not transferred to her late husband's account. Instead the amount was transferred to some DEAF account. At that time, I was new to banking, and the concept of DEAF was not familiar to me so I researched more about it. During my research, I learned that since the FD was more than 10 years old and no family member has claimed the amount, it had been transferred to RBI in its DEAF account. Subsequently, I initiated the claim process, and after completing the required documentation, the lady received the funds a few days later.

The reason for sharing this incident is that a lot of money is still lying unclaimed with banks, insurance companies, share market and other financial institutions. According to a report published in a leading newspaper, a huge sum of Rs. 1,50,000 crore is still lying unclaimed in India as of December-2020. This chapter is dedicated to understanding how to avoid such mistakes and the methods to track and retrieve the unclaimed amounts. To do that, we must first understand why the investment remains unclaimed with financial institutions. The following are the reasons for this:

1) KYC -Most of the unclaimed deposits, especially in banks are not KYC compliant. The KYC documents such as identity proof and address proof provided are often outdated. Current mobile numbers are also not provided, which makes it difficult for the banks to contact the customers. Therefore, it is advised to submit the KYC details at regular intervals. In particular, ensure that your current mobile number is updated for all your investment products so that financial institutions can be able to contact you regarding any updates of your investments.

2) Nomination - While making any investment, a nominee should always be assigned to that investment. In the event of unfortunate demise of the investor, the nominee can easily file a claim and receive the amount. If the nomination is not done, a long and complex documentation process is to be followed, which requires presence of all the legal heirs to claim the amount. If there is no consensus among the legal heirs, the matter may even go to court, and the amount remains unclaimed till the time the court order is issued. All such issues can be avoided by assigning a nominee.

3) Transfer / Change of Address -In the event of shifting to a new city, it is important to transfer all your accounts to the nearby branch of the new city and update the new address in your accounts. It helps you to keep track of your accounts and financial institutions can also correspond with you easily. The process of account transfer is very simple and can also be done with the help of internet-banking.

4) Recordkeeping - A file or record should be maintained which contains the details of all the investments. Such records shall be updated regularly, and the information of such investment should be shared with the family members. One of the main reasons for unclaimed amount is that the family members are often unaware of the investments, making it difficult for them to claim them. The file or record should contain the details of all your bank accounts, FD receipts, shares, MFs, bonds, policy papers, locker details, property papers and any other investments. This practice can help the family members to track all the investments effortlessly.

It may also happen that, there are some investments a person has forgotten about, or a person is now deceased, and the family members are unaware of their investments. We will see how to trace these investments and the ways of making a claim:

1) In today's digital age, most of the investments are done online, hence these investment products can be tracked from the mobile phone. Family members can check the financial apps and log in to view investment portfolio. SMS alerts received can also be checked to identify the financial data. Along with this, e-mails should also be accessed to check for any e-statements received from financial institutions.
2) Bank statements and previous income tax returns should also be checked for any investment-related details contained therein.
3) Right to Information (RTI) can also be filed to get information from various financial institutions for information regarding the investments. RTI can also be filed to gather information regarding any property details owned by the person with the relevant registrar's office.
4) When an amount remains unclaimed for more than 10 years in banks, it is transferred to RBI in its fund called Depositor's Education and Awareness Fund (DEAF). RBI has mandated banks to publish the record of accounts whose amount has been transferred to the DEAF account. To access these details, you can check the official website of bank and check the details of inoperative/unclaimed deposits. It can also be checked from a simple Google enquiry for each bank. For example, if you want to search the record of inoperative/unclaimed deposits of say HDFC bank, you can search it by typing "HDFC unclaimed deposits" on Google and a link of that bank will appear. You can

search the records by putting in name and other details of the investor. If any matching details are found, an application can be submitted to the bank along with the necessary documents to claim the amount.

5) The unclaimed amounts of insurance, PPF, NSC, KVP, SSA, post office deposits are transferred to the Senior Citizens' Welfare Fund (SCWF). Like bank deposits, here also a Google search can be done to track the investment details.
6) Similar to DEAF, if dividends from shares remain unclaimed for more than 7 years, these shares are transferred to Investor Education and Protection Fund (IEPF). The details of such shares can be accessed from the portal https://iepf.gov.in. The relevant forms for claim processing can also be downloaded from the portal. Mutual Funds and other market-related products can be tracked down from the websites of the respective financial institutions by providing the necessary details of the investor.

These are the methods by which unclaimed amounts can be tracked claimed. I hope it will help the investors and their families retrieve their money, which can create a sound financial legacy for future generations. With this, we have finished the final chapter of the book.

GETTING FINANCIALLY INDEPENDENT

Money is an interesting thing. It is never enough and it is always enough. The sufficiency of money often depends on our spending habits. As our income grows, we tend to spend more which in turn leads to a mis-balanced financial life. However, when faced with challenging circumstances, we manage with whatever money we have. There are thousand ways to spend money but very few ways a person earns money. Hence it becomes important to restrict ourselves from spending money on unnecessary things.

One prominent rule, recommended by many educators is that the income should be divided into 3 parts, in the ratio of 50:30:20. According to this rule, 50% of the income should be allocated for basic needs such as rent/EMI, groceries and other household expenses. 30% should be set aside for wants such as vacations, shopping, movies, or other enjoyable activities. The remaining 20% should be dedicated to savings and investments for the future. In this way, you can manage your lifestyle and also have savings for the future. You can either follow this rule or create your own based on your preference and circumstances. Young people can save more than 20% as they do not have much responsibility. However, as we grow older, you have to spend more on the needs. But the important thing is to create the goals. Once you have fixed your goals, you need to determine the amount required for fulfilling the goal, and the number of years to achieve it. With that, you can select the type and the amount of investment.

In this book, we have covered the basics of investments, loans, insurance products along with other financial instruments. Once you have grasped the basic concepts, it becomes easier to do deep research into that product. It will help you to choose a better product as you have all the relevant information with you.

I believe the ultimate goal of human life should be to pursue our passions. But unfortunately, we cannot do that due to lack of money and time. Most of our time is spent in earning money. Therefore, achieving financial independence becomes crucial for a happy life. But what exactly does financial independence mean? For instance, if we invest Rs. 1 crore in a product like fixed deposit or pension plan with a 7% interest rate, it would generate a monthly income of Rs. 58,000, that too for a lifetime. It means we would receive a regular monthly income without having to work another day. Therefore, financial independence is where money works for you, rather than you working for money. This passive income can enable us to follow our passion or hobbies which we had to forgo due to our busy life. All it takes is to plan and invest properly to make that corpus which will give us stress-free life and an ample amount of time.

With this, we conclude the book and hope that it will help you to take better financial decisions and have a prosperous fulfilling life. Wish you a happy and financially secure future.

For any queries or feedback, you can contact us on kyfinance101@gmail.com or visit our Facebook/Twitter page "Know Your Finance" for more updates.